Howard Hughes

The Pocket Essential

SPAGHETTI WESTERNS

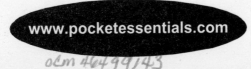

www.pocketessentials.com

First published in Great Britain 2001 by Pocket Essentials, 18 Coleswood Road, Harpenden, Herts, AL5 1EQ

Distributed in the USA by Trafalgar Square Publishing, PO Box 257, Howe Hill Road, North Pomfret, Vermont 05053

A CIP catalogue record for this book is available from the British Library.

ISBN 1-903047-42-0

9 8 7 6 5 4 3 2 1

Book typeset by Pdunk
Printed and bound by Cox & Wyman

for Barbara

Acknowledgements

Thanks to Paul Duncan, Alex (for additional research), Is, Mum and Dad, Belinda, René, Lionel Woodman, Dave, Ion, Jez, Ann, Nicki, John, Bob, Sonya, and especially to Clara, all of whom have contributed to the writing of this book.

CONTENTS

Spaghetti Westerns: Introducing The Gang

The storekeeper looked up. Silhouetted in the open doorway stood a man, his face hidden by the lowered brim of his battered Stetson. The stranger paused to take a long drag on the cigar clenched between his teeth, as he slowly raised his head to stare at the proprietor. The storekeeper caught sight of the stranger's stubbled, sunburnt face and his piercing, cold eyes. Ominously, with the clink of spurs, the figure walked to the counter. Unnerved, a bead of sweat rolled down the storekeeper's brow as he spluttered, "What…er…what can I get you sir?" For a moment, the stranger held his gaze in silence. Then he replied in a low whispering drawl, "Do you have *A Bullet For The General* or *A Pistol For Ringo*?" The storekeeper looked perplexed. "I'm sorry…We don't sell guns sir", he answered, "This is a video shop."

Spaghetti Westerns - their style has passed into cinematic folklore, their heroes have become superstars and their influential music has become instantly recognisable. Cool gringos and stone-faced bounty hunters shot Mexican bandits for fistfuls of dollars, in the bleakest of desert landscapes. Striding way over the line normally called self-parody, Italian-made Spaghetti Westerns are the most enduringly popular genre to have emerged from Cinecittà Film Studios in Rome. Through their mannered style, rejection of Hollywood clichés, amazingly influential music, sharp editing and pared-down dialogue they are, with the James Bond movies, the brutal model for sixties action cinema. Cinema and TV audiences the world over are familiar with Clint Eastwood's poncho-clad, cigar-chewing drifter, making his image the enduring symbol of the genre. A man alone (or occasionally in an untrustworthy partnership) facing villains that are irredeemably bad. Eastwood killed with a speed and detachment never seen before on the cinema screen. He was the epitome of cool, a man of few words and even fewer morals, who would sell his gun to the highest bidder in an effort to get rich in a desolate wasteland - where dollars meant everything and life meant nothing.

As directed by visionary Italian director Sergio Leone in the plains of Spain, Eastwood became the ultimate anti-hero and their three films together, *A Fistful Of Dollars* (1964), *For A Few Dollars More* (1965) and *The Good, The Bad And The Ugly* (1966) - dubbed the 'Dollars Trilogy' - were hugely successful, making Eastwood the biggest star of his generation and arguably (John Wayne fans would disagree) the most famous movie gunslinger of them all. Leone directed two more Westerns, but the runaway success of his movies, in particular the Eastwood films, led to all the other foreign Westerns (between 1961 and 1978 there were 500 made) being universally disregarded as worthless copyists. Most of the Italian, German, Spanish and French Westerns made throughout the sixties were rightly labelled junk. But this vast output is now more accessible, due to the films' availability on video, so Western fans can at last make up their own minds. Of the numerous Spaghettis made, there are at least 20 films that deserve the kudos of Leone's movies. And there are plenty that were considerably more appealing and contemporary than John Wayne wandering through Texas telling everyone to vote Republican. Because Eastwood became a star, the films directed by Leone's cohorts, rivals and in some cases friends have been largely ignored in mainstream circles, even though some of their films, particularly the comedy Spaghetti Westerns, went on to make more money than Leone's films.

The time has come to set things aright.

European Westerns?

Westerns were one of the most popular forms of cinema entertainment ever. Even now TV schedules are packed with all sorts of Westerns. Many excellent examples had been made in the first part of the twentieth century by masterly practitioners like John Ford, Raoul Walsh and Howard Hawks, but the vast majority were program fillers, singing cowboy vehicles (usually accompanied by a horse as a sidekick) and serial Westerns - fast, action-filled oaters aimed at the matinee audience. But by the fifties the subtext had deepened, with more thought being given even to the low-budget B-Westerns. Subjects like racism, delinquency, McCarthyism and psychology were often injected into the scenarios. But because of the shear volume of B-Westerns being produced, audiences were getting fed up with the same plots and actors cropping up over and over again. After all, they could get that on TV.

The emergence of the TV Western in the mid-fifties was the death knell of the Hollywood Western. The big cinema hits were super productions like *Ben Hur* and *El Cid*, giant movies on giant screens, with stars like Charlton Heston and Sophia Loren. If you wanted to see a Western, you tuned in to *Gunsmoke*, *Laramie* or *Rawhide* once a week, to see what Chuck, Hank or Rowdy were up to. Meanwhile, popular Western themes were appearing elsewhere - the prime example are the films of Japanese director Akira Kurosawa. His *Seven Samurai* (1954) was obviously influenced by classic Hollywood Westerns. For poor peasant farmers read poor settlers, for roving bandits read roving Indians and for Seven Samurai read the Seventh Cavalry. *Yojimbo* (1961) and *Sanjuro* (1962) looked even more like Westerns, especially *Yojimbo* with its windswept ghost town and warring gangs. Stylistically, emotionally and technically these intelligent action movies were way ahead of the field. In 1960 *Seven Samurai* became the basis for *The Magnificent Seven*, a hugely successful Western, which made its best box-office returns not in America, but in Europe.

Curiously, with less real Westerns being released countries that liked Westerns, but weren't getting any decent ones, decided to manufacture their own. Rising production costs were one of the deciding factors in reducing the number of American Westerns produced, but costs in Europe were considerably less. Spain was an exceptionally cheap location for making exotic desert-set action movies. In the late fifties and early sixties the Spaniards and British started making Westerns in the sun-scorched landscape of Almeria, Southern Spain. The Americans soon followed suit. It was an irony that it was cheaper to make Westerns in this ersatz West than it was to film them in the real thing.

Even weirder was when the West Germans joined in, using Yugoslavia as the American frontier. German author Karl May was long dead when director Harald Reinl decided to film May's 'Winnetou' stories in 1962. The series concerned the adventures of a buckskinned adventurer Old Shatterhand (Lex Barker) and his Tonto-like sidekick Apache chief Winnetou (Pierre Brice). The series began with the action-packed *The Treasure Of Silver Lake*, with Herbert Lom (from the Inspector Clouseau films) as the villain. Making a killing in Europe, the sequel *Winnetou The Warrior* (1963) was even more successful. Other notable examples included *Last Of The Renegades* (1964) with Klaus Kinski as a baddie in a coonskin hat, and *Among Vultures* (1964) with English actor Stewart Granger playing effete Old Surehand. The action sequences were impressively staged and remain the most memorable aspects of the series - from massed attacks on forts, towns and Indian villages, burning oil wells and wagon train massacres to more unusual action spots like bear wrestling and trains driven through saloons. Martin Böttcher's music was suitably epic (with a resonance that sounded like it was recorded in an echo chamber) and the films revitalised hackneyed Western plots - something that Hollywood had presumed impossible in the early sixties.

Italia Film Presenta - The Glory Days Of Cinecittà

The Italian film industry in the late fifties, throughout the sixties and into the early seventies was the most magical and exciting film factory in the world, if only for the sheer volume and diversity of its product that swamped cinemas across the globe. Based at Cinecittà Studios in Rome, the studio dabbled in every popular genre and added its own peculiar edge to imported ideas. Every few years a new fad would catch the public's attention and clean up at the box office until interest waned. The first Italian genre to transcend domestic success was the Muscleman Epics in the late fifties. Starring American and British ex-bodybuilders and lifeguards like Steve Reeves, Reg Park and Gordon Scott, as mythical strongmen named Hercules and Goliath, these way out fantasies (with strong homo-erotic undertones) were amazingly popular in Europe. The best of these movies are highly camp, mythical adventures with ridiculous special effects, monsters of the 'man-in-a-suit' variety and very wooden acting. But they were a breath of fresh air when compared to Hollywood's straight-faced treatment of similar subjects. During the Muscleman fad (which ran from 1958-66), several other popular films series came and went. These included pirate escapades, Viking Sagas, period swashbucklers, sexy shockumentaries and Sci-Fi films. Moreover, genre cross-pollination occasionally produced bizarre results - Sci-Fi Horror Movies, Swashbuckling Musclemen and Viking Horrors. And all of these myriad genres were then set up by the bumbling, slapstick comedians of the day - Franchi and Ingrassi, and Totò.

But in the sixties, three subjects dominated Italian production - Horror, Spies and Westerns. The Italian Horror cycle, started by Mario Bava's *Mask Of Satan* (1960, starring Barbara Steele) brought new life to the undead. Bava and company produced some truly imaginative, darkly twisted period Gothic Horrors - exquisite, stylish movies that used swathes of gaudy colours or the menacing shadows of black and white to startling effect. British actress Steele became the star of the genre. This series anticipated the 'Giallo' slasher cycle in the seventies. The Italian Spy movies were copies of the Bond movies, detailing outlandish international espionage, global villainy and flashy gadgets. Exotic locations, from snowbound Austria to sweltering Egypt, were cheaply created via stock footage.

Italian Westerns

The most financially successful, innovative and influential of these crazes was the Italian 'Spaghetti' Western, also referred to as Macaroni, Pizza, Pasta or Paella Westerns ('Paella' for the Spanish involvement). Italians called them Western All'Italiana (Italian-Style Westerns), but to aficionados these days they're more often called Euro-Westerns (which includes Italian, British, Spanish, French and German productions). When the musclemen lost their strength at the box office and the American production companies pulled out of Italy (after a series of big-budget financial disasters) the search was on for a new genre to hijack. With the series of Westerns being made in Spain by the Spanish, French and British, and the runaway success of the German Winnetou films, the Italian movie industry began to experiment with Westerns of their own. Initially they invested in the Winnetou series in co-production deals, but realised that Spanish participation would make more sense locationwise, film crewwise and extrawise. Early Italian examples followed the Winnetou movies with the Cavalry and Indians scenario, epitomised by *Buffalo Bill - Hero Of The Far West* (1964). But soon the genre changed tack and the Spanish desert became the American Southwest of Arizona, Texas and New Mexico. And instead of warpaint and feathers, extras found themselves donning sombreros, bandoleers and some heavy hardware.

A Stranger In Town - Lone Hero Spaghettis

The most important and trendsetting Italian Western was *A Fistful Of Dollars*, made in the summer of 1964. Directed by Italian Sergio Leone and starring American TV actor (then unknown on celluloid) Clint Eastwood, the movie instantly established a new style of Western. Eastwood was sick of the plot constraints of his Western TV series *Rawhide* and Leone was eager to update the Western myth for the James Bond generation. More intelligently, he later claimed that his aim in his early Westerns was to combine the imagery of the silent film with Neo-Realism. He also wanted to rid the West of all the talky characters and the women (who slowed down the plot), and concentrate on the important stuff, like fast action and money. And the one thing that cinema-released Westerns could still give the public was violence, because TV was under censorship restrictions (guardianship of the young and all that). Continental cinema had always been a little more adventurous with its action, so when Leone made his first Western, he laced his story with much violent gunplay, fist-

11

icuffs and cruel action (with death by shotgun, machete, machine-gun and incineration).

In Eastwood, Leone found the perfect hero-figure for his Western fantasies. Eastwood, as 'The Man With No Name', looked like no other Western hero who had preceded him. He wore a Mexican poncho, permanently smoked cigars, rode a mule and his ruthless speed with a gun made him the fastest man around. He is the ultimate cool gunfighter, who rides into a town run by two rival gangs and makes a killing out of the conflict of interests by hiring himself as a mercenary to each side in turn. The villains were played by Italian, Spanish and West German actors, the supporting cast came from as far afield as Austria and America - a truly cosmopolitan production. To hide this from European audiences, cast and crew often used American-sounding pseudonyms. The music was written by Italian Ennio Morricone, who conceived a strange echoing backdrop to the desolate action - all whip cracks, whistles, electric guitars and trumpet flourishes. If the dialogue in *A Fistful Of Dollars* was sparse, Leone intended Morricone's music to fill in the emotional gaps in a bizarre variation of Robert Browning's famous quote: "Who hears music feels his solitude peopled at once." Judging by the number of lone heroes that followed in Eastwood's wake, it's lucky Morricone's music was around to keep them company.

In *A Fistful Of Dollars*, all the Spaghetti Western ingredients were in place. The sunny locale, the whitewashed village, vicious moustachioed bandits, a señorita in peril and most importantly the lone hero, who doesn't need no one, and lives nowhere. Invariably the hero is warned to leave town and equally invariably he ignores the advice and gets involved in the ensuing carnage. In the numerous *A Fistful Of Dollars* clones the hero usually ends up facing the villain and his gang in a deserted, windblown Mexican street. There is an all-consuming silence, periodically interrupted by the crunch of boots and the clink of spurs, as the adversaries square up for the showdown. Long stares and huge close-ups reinforce the static, threatening moment before death, when a bead of sweat or a twitchy trigger-finger take on the significance of a paragraph of dialogue. Then, in a moment, the guns are drawn, bullets fly and the villains lie dead. Flies buzz in for a feast, as the hero spits into the dust, stares at the riddled corpses with contempt and allows himself a sneer of satisfaction.

Nobody did it better than Eastwood but, with the success of *A Fistful Of Dollars*, many imitators followed. The most blatant was Tony Anthony's 'Stranger' trilogy. Most of the early Spaghettis used the lone gunman scenario, arriving in a variety of towns (ghost town, boom town, gold town, crooked town) and combating the local hoods - bandits, bankers, cattle rustlers, outlaws or embezzlers - in their own inimitable way. Producers soon realised that every gunman should have a gimmick and that's when things got really interesting.

Romance On The Range - Idealism Goes West

The other most important hero of this early part of the Spaghetti boom was Ringo, as played by Italian actor Giuliano Gemma. In contrast to Eastwood's taciturn drifter, Ringo was altogether more talkative. Also, director Duccio Tessari wasn't keen to emulate the style of *A Fistful Of Dollars*, even though he had contributed to Leone's script. Instead, he attempted a purer homage to the Hollywood masters and also to the serial Westerns of the forties. His first attempt at this resulted in *A Pistol For Ringo* (1965), a tension-filled, well-plotted Western that was a world away from Leone's vision of the West as wasteland. Tessari adapted the classic siege scenario (a gang of bandits hide out at a ranch after a bungled robbery and take an innocent family prisoner) and then had clean-cut, wisecracking gunman Ringo infiltrate the ranch and save the hostages. The success of this movie led to an immediate sequel *The Return Of Ringo* (1965) - a Westernised version of Homer's *The Odyssey* - which was much darker and more complex than the first movie. With these films, Gemma became a popular hero, though he had already experimented with the Ringo persona in *One Silver Dollar* the previous year. These lyrical entries weren't as violent as Leone's Westerns and harked back to Hollywood for inspiration - *The Return Of Ringo* included references to Howard Hawks, John Ford and John Sturges. Moreover, the soundtrack often featured a crooning ballad, further reinforcing the films' Hollywood origins.

Untrustworthy Alliances - Gunslingers Team Up

While Ringo extolled the virtues of honour and trust, and everyone else tried to remake *A Fistful Of Dollars*, Leone's next Western expanded the lone gunman formula. Via *For A Few Dollars More*, the next schema to emerge was based on the reasoning - double the heroes, double the action. Hopefully that also meant double the audience. For Leone, who had removed women from his West altogether, the only way to get any kind of relationships into his films was to give his hero a sidekick. In this sequel he teamed Eastwood with Lee Van Cleef (a bit player in fifties Westerns) as Colonel Mortimer, an aged, black-clad, professional bounty hunter. This teaming was one of the most influential moments in the genre. Even in the seventies, directors were still making movies about the 'old man' joining forces with a 'boy', the generation gap (a sense of the 'good old days') adding to the relationship. Van Cleef based much of his career on this schema. He was teamed with a younger man in many of his Westerns, including *Death Rides A Horse* (1967) and *Day Of Anger* (1967). One of the strangest aspects of Spaghetti Westerns is that actors are yoked together in an endless mix-and-match effort to get bigger audiences. If a duo worked well together, there was the guarantee of sequels and spin-offs. A mixture of actors also gave the producers a range of options when publicising the film. To take one example - when *Day Of Anger* (starring Van Cleef and Gemma) was released in the UK, Van Cleef was the star, but in Spain and Italy Gemma was top-billed. Over the years bounty hunters teamed up to catch outlaws, outlaws teamed up to kill bounty hunters, Indians helped white men, etc... As the genre rolled on, the groups of heroes got bigger, trading on the success of *The Magnificent Seven*. Often a group of experts would get together for a special job (steal a train, get revenge on a bandit), each member characterised by his particular skill - knife-throwing, dynamite, strength, brains - and each would get an opportunity to make their skill count, as in *Kill Them All And Come Back Alone* (1968) and *The Five Man Army* (1969).

'Didn't You Kill My Brother?' - Tales Of Revenge

The sub-plot of *For A Few Dollars More* featured Van Cleef's Colonel tracking down his sister's killer. Throughout the film, this motive is concealed from the audience - only a flashback at the end and a brief line of dialogue reveal that the bandit El Indio was responsible for her death. Revenge was by far the most popular motive for Italian Western heroes. Vengeance was often integrated into other scenarios (the lone gunman scenario, a political outline) and involved the hero searching for whoever killed his wife/mother/father/sister/brother/son/daughter/friend/business partner/entire family/entire tribe or entire home town - delete where applicable. Other revenge scenarios based themselves on crippling injuries incurred on the hero years before, like the marksman shot in both hands and unable to hold a pistol in *Bandidos* (1967). The best revenge Spaghettis are *For A Few Dollars More*, Lizzani's *The Hills Run Red* (an update of Anthony Mann's psychotic Westerns made with James Stewart), *Django* (mud-strewn, Civil War revenge), *Navajo Joe* (racist vengeance), *Death Rides A Horse* (family revenge) and *Once Upon A Time In The West* (brotherly revenge), though dozens of variations were released.

14

Get A Coffin Ready - Enter Django And The Gravediggers

Sergio Corbucci made *Django* (1966) as an attempt to create the ultimate anti-hero. He wanted his West to be the antithesis of Leone, even though the plot was a retread of *A Fistful Of Dollars*. No sunshine, no sand, just mud, rain and blood. The protagonists were dressed in rags, the town looked like a ruin and the hero was crippled before the final shootout. Franco Nero played Django and became an international star, but it was the distinctive clothes and props that audiences remembered. Django is dressed in a long Union coat, black clothes, fingerless gloves and a scarf, like an Army gravedigger. Behind him he dragged a coffin through the mud. Inside the box is his weapon of choice - a belt-feed machine-gun. With the film's astonishing success came the inevitable imitators, most of whom simply used the Django name (like *Django Kill*) - the majority have nothing to do with the original. The two Django movies really worth looking out for are *Django Get A Coffin Ready* (1968) and *Django The Bastard* (1969), both of which are remarkably close to Corbucci's movie. In 1968, Sartana appeared on the scene. A more suave version of Django, he kick-started a series of his own which ran into the early seventies. Sartana referred to himself as a pall-bearer, while Django was a gravedigger, though both were equally lethal. The Sartana cycle was more consistent, with the hero's character remaining constant for the series and actor Gianni Garko playing him in most entries.

Viva La Revolución! - Spaghettis With A Conscience

From 1966 more astute Italian producers and directors realised that they could make a political statement at the same time as a few million lira if they infused their Westerns with a little ideology. The first to try this was Damiano Damiani with his Mexican Revolution tale of greed and betrayal *A Bullet For The General* (1966). Relatively few serious Mexican Revolution Political Spaghettis followed, because the accent shifted to send-up. Influenced by Brigitte Bardot's musical comedy *Viva Maria* (1965), Corbucci made the best of the less than serious Political movies - *A Professional Gun* (1968). Sergio Sollima also made a significant contribution to the genre, but set his Westerns, *The Big Gundown* (1966) and *Face To Face* (1967), in the American Southwest. His political figures were lawmen, Mexican bandits, college professors and railroad magnets, which often led to a clash between culture and ignorance, honesty and lies. Both the serious and the send-ups featured a relationship between a Mexican peasant and a foreigner, often a European mercenary, but in some of the more offbeat examples the peasant is teamed with an English doctor, a Dutch oil explorer, a Russian prince or an Italian Shakespearean actor. The relationship between the two men was supposed to echo the relationship between the capitalist powers and the relative poverty of the Third World, though often the films were an excuse for a lot of over-the-top action.

Epic Landscapes - Big-Budget Spaghettis

As Spaghettis became extremely successful, the need for co-production deals faded. Many of the big-budget Spaghettis after 1966 were solely Italian productions. Others like Leone's *The Good, The Bad And The Ugly* were part-financed by United Artists, even before *A Fistful Of Dollars* and *For A Few Dollars More* had been released in the States. United Artists had bought the rights to the Dollars films and with the Bond movies, they cleaned up as the most astute US studio of the sixties. In 1968 (the year *The Good, The Bad And The Ugly* was released stateside) UA made over $20 million in profit - an all time high. *The Good, The Bad And The Ugly* provided a memorable backdrop to the story, with its re-creation of the American Civil War. Leone then made *Once Upon A Time In The West* (1968) part-financed by Paramount Studios and cast stars like Henry Fonda, Jason Robards and Claudia Cardinale. *Once Upon A Time* didn't bear any resemblance to the cheap shoot-em-ups cartwheeling off the Cinecittà conveyor belt, but looked rather like the epic Hollywood Westerns of Ford, De Mille and Wyler. Leone was able to include scenes of the railroad moving West towards the Pacific, a thriving boom town and even location footage shot in Monument Valley, Ford's favourite location. The increased Italian budgets also enabled Corbucci to convincingly recreate the Mexican Revolution in *A Professional Gun* and *Compañeros*, Tonino Valerii to depict Post-Civil War Dallas in *The Price Of Power* and Leone to hire big-name stars like Rod Steiger and James Coburn for his last Western, *Duck You Sucker* (1971). The cycle came full circle when British and American film-makers arrived in Spain in the late sixties to make their own blockbuster variations of Spaghetti Westerns, starring superstars like Robert Mitchum, Sean Connery and Oliver Reed, which were generally inferior to the genuine article.

Seesaws And Quick-Draws - Circus Westerns

With more Spaghettis being made, the competition became tougher. There were epileptic gunmen, one-armed gunmen, gunslinger-priests, gunslinger-florists, amnesiac gunmen, albino gunmen, blind gunmen, deaf gunmen, mute gunmen and homosexual mercenaries, armed with everything from knives to Gatling guns. There were Horror Westerns, Thriller Westerns and Musical Westerns, the latter exemplified by *Little Rita Of The West* (1967), which starts as a straightforward Spaghetti until an appalling Eurovision song blasts out of nowhere and the cast start singing and dancing. By far the most popular of these offbeat diversions were the Acrobatic Westerns directed by Gianfranco Parolini, who managed to get acrobats and stunts into his scenarios, whatever the genre. His best Westerns, starring Lee Van Cleef as the black-clad, ex-Confederate Major named Sabata, incorporated many gadgets into the action - gimmicky weapons, magnetic cigars, seesaws (to gain access to a bank) - making their action set pieces extraordinarily imaginative. The first one, *Sabata* (1969), was the best, though there were many examples, including several actually set in a travelling circus, like *Boot Hill* (1969) and *The Return Of Sabata* (1971). The formula was updated in the seventies to incorporate Kung-Fu action into the mix, in East-meets-West movies like *Blood Money* (1973).

Pasta Joke - Comic Spaghettis

By 1970 the violence in Italian Westerns had escalated dramatically and just about every single Western avenue had been explored. With audiences tiring of such savagery, there seemed nowhere for the Spaghetti Westerns to go. In 1967 an enterprising director named Giuseppe Collizi teamed a handsome blond leading man named 'Terence Hill' (real name Mario Girotti) with hulking, Bluto-like 'Bud Spencer' (or Carlo Pedersoli) as the heroes in *God Forgives - I Don't*, which spawned two sequels (*Ace High* and *Boot Hill*). Enzo Barboni, an ex-cameraman, was looking to move into directing and hired the duo to star in his second directorial effort. Entitled *They Call Me Trinity*, the film cast Hill and Spencer as unlikely brothers, Trinity and Bambino, in a light-hearted, clever parody of *The Magnificent Seven* and Westerns by Leone and Sollima. A runaway success at the box office, it led to an even more successful sequel *Trinity Is Still My Name* (1971) that out-grossed Leone's Dollars movies. The films lampooned Western myths, including live action cartoon fist fights, speeded-up gunfights, drunken monks, sexy Mormon girls and farting babies in an uproarious send-up of the genre. As to be expected, there was the usual slew of imitators (which did wonders for the Italian breakaway furniture trade), but as the humour got cruder and more laboured, the comedy cycle spluttered, prompting Hill and Spencer to adapt their Trinity double act in contemporary settings in a series of clodhopping comedies, which achieved the impossible and made the Trinity films look subtle.

Sundowner

By the early seventies, the Italian Western had run its course. The most popular Italian films of the period were the Gialli (supernatural chillers and slasher movies pioneered by Dario Argento) and ultra-violent Thrillers, continental versions of lone-cop scenarios like *The French Connection* and *Dirty Harry*. The last great Spaghetti Westerns bore little resemblance to the Dollars films that had popularised the genre. In 1973 Tonino Valerii directed *My Name Is Nobody*, an analysis of the relationship between Hollywood Westerns (epitomised in the film by Henry Fonda's ageing shootist) and their rougher Spaghetti cousins (represented by Terence Hill, who affords Fonda heroic status). The film even mocked Sam Peckinpah's take on the Western, with a host of in-jokes. The last gasp of the genre were the mystical, misty 'Twilight' Spaghettis like *Keoma* (1976), films that adopted a primitive, elemental approach to Westerns and addressed such subjects as racism with an incisiveness rarely seen in the genre. This wasn't enough to save the cycle and though there have been Spaghetti Westerns made since, and many American Westerns ripped off the Italian style, the heyday had passed.

Rogues Gallery

Clint Eastwood remains the best-known Spaghetti Western hero, followed closely by Lee Van Cleef. This pair epitomised everything that the Italian West had come to symbolise - cool gunmen, stylish clothes, taciturn manner and the ability to kill half a dozen bandits without blinking an eye. But the Italian Western craze created a whole wagonload of stars, as actors of all nationalities flocked to Cinecittà to get a piece of the gunslinger action. Luminaries such as Orson Welles, Joseph Cotton and James Mason appeared in films that they hoped would never be released in their native countries, while everyone from William Shatner and Burt Reynolds to Henry Fonda and James Garner travelled to Spain to try their hands at Spaghettis. The Italian-style Western also made stars of many fifties Hollywood B-Western villains, like Lee Van Cleef, Jack Palance and Henry Silva. It revitalised the careers of actors on the wane, including Cameron Mitchell, Dan Duryea, John Ireland and Farley Granger, though their turns were often as plausible as Terry-Thomas playing a Mexican bandit. But the rejection of Hollywood stereotypes appealed to actors who had been shot at for years by bland heroes, and Van Cleef and Palance in particular were pleased to offer a different side to the story. Most of all it created a slew of new cosmopolitan stars whose looks, whether good, bad or ugly, lent themselves to these macabre tales. Actors like Franco Nero (the original Django), pretty boy Giuliano Gemma (angel-faced Ringo), Terence Hill (dusty-but-charming Trinity), Cuban Che Guevara lookalike Tomas Milian, German gargoyle Klaus Kinski and Spaniard Fernando Sancho (who made a living as a swaggering moustachioed Mexican bandido) became massive stars, especially in Europe, the Far East and the Third World. Everywhere in fact except Britain and the States, though Kinski did eventually break through to critical acclaim outside Europe when he started working for Werner Herzog on *Aguirre Wrath Of God* (1973). Interestingly, actors who made their names in Spaghettis and later moved on to pastures new periodically referred to their Western roots, no matter how clumsy the context - like Eastwood facing a Tiger tank in a Spaghetti Western duel during the WW2 adventure *Kelly's Heroes* (1970) and Terence Hill in a gundown pastiche on motorbikes in *Watch Out, We're Mad!* (1973).

Music Maestro

Outside of Clint Eastwood's stubble and blanket, Lee Van Cleef's grim face and the stylised gunfights, the musical scores that accompany Spaghetti Westerns are the most memorable aspect of the genre. They captured the mood of the Spaghetti West perfectly, as well as being extremely influential on popular culture, extending beyond Westerns and into pop music and advertising. The most important musical figure of the period was Ennio Morricone, a classically-trained composer and an old school friend of Leone's. Born on 10th November 1928, Morricone attended the Santa Cecilia Conservatory in Rome, studying composition, musical direction, choral work and trumpet (his father played the instrument in cabaret). But while Morricone studied he also played his trumpet in nightclubs (sometimes subbing for his father) and began honing his composition and arranging skills on standards of the day. Upon graduation he decided to move into the lucrative record industry, arranging pop records for popular artists like Mario Lanza and Paul Anka, before eventually expanding his repertoire to composing and arranging for radio, TV and theatre. His distinctive pop style can be heard to best advantage on Mina's 1966 hit 'Se Telefonando' (co-written by Morricone for an Italian TV show), which sounds like a cross between a Burt Bacharach ballad, Phil

Spector's 'Wall Of Sound' and the epic quality found in Morricone's Western scores. His popularity in the pop industry (and the tag 'the father of modern arrangement') inevitably led to film work in the early sixties and brought him into contact with Leone, who was preparing *A Fistful Of Dollars*. Morricone had already scored a Spaghetti Western in 1963 (*Gunfight In The Red Sands*) and was signed to work on another called *Bullets Don't Argue* (1964). Both movies had used the same Spanish locations as *A Fistful Of Dollars*, but that was where any similarity ended.

Although Leone was unimpressed by Morricone's early Western scores, Morricone was nevertheless hired to concoct a score for *A Fistful Of Dollars*. Initial pieces proffered by the composer were vetoed by Leone, until Morricone played him an unusual arrangement of 'Pastures Of Plenty', a Woody Guthrie song re-voiced by Peter Tevis. Leone liked it and decided to use the piece (minus the vocals) with a whistler replacing Tevis. Employing Alessandro Alessandroni to whistle and play guitar, an orchestra and Alessandroni's choir, 'I Cantori Moderni' ('The Modern Singers'), Morricone produced the most amazing theme tune. With its whiplashes, bells, electric guitar (very similar to Hank Marvin's Shadows-style tremolo) and an eerie whistled melody, the piece instantly evoked a Western setting. It was also refreshingly simple and highly catchy - almost like a pop single. In fact, many of Morricone's subsequent singles and albums were hugely successful in Italy, while a cover version of his theme from *The Good, The Bad And The Ugly* by Hugo Montenegro topped the UK charts in 1968. It is interesting that the two most innovative film composers for action films in the sixties, Morricone and the Bond films' John Barry, both made their names with distinctive arrangements of other people's work. Barry created the famous 'James Bond Theme' by reworking Monty Norman's original composition and augmented it with his own 'Bees Knees' instrumental, though Barry has since sought sole authorship of the tune. It seems that just about every aspect of *A Fistful Of Dollars* had a source elsewhere. But when these myriad influences converged (Eastwood's image, Leone's artistry, Morricone's musicianship), they created startling effects.

With the success of the *A Fistful Of Dollars* score, Morricone soon became synonymous with Italian-style Westerns and his music became a major contributing factor to their popularity. The following year he worked for Leone on *For A Few Dollars More*, creating an even better backdrop to the action, whilst also scoring Tessari's Ringo films, with compositions that echoed his work in the pop industry. The title songs of both the Ringo movies were voiced in English (even in the Italian print) by Maurizio Graf. But between 1966 and 1969 Morricone was incredibly prolific and wrote for many of the most financially successful Spaghettis of the day. Sometimes (as in the case of *A Bullet For The General* and *Fort Yuma Gold*) he worked in collaboration with other composers. Sometimes he used pseudonyms to conceal his prodigious output. On *A Fistful Of Dollars* he called himself 'Dan Savio' to fall in line with the rest of the production, but on *The Hills Run Red*, *Navajo Joe* and *The Hellbenders* he worked as 'Leo Nichols' (a moniker he often used to conduct his own scores). He composed many of his scores, but they were conducted by his assistant Bruno Nicolai, who moved into composing in the mid-sixties. Morricone worked as well with Tessari, Sollima (*The Big Gundown* and *Face To Face*) and Corbucci (*Navajo Joe*, *The Big Silence* and *A Professional Gun*) as he did with Leone, with much less recognition. By the time these films were released outside Europe (in the late sixties and early seventies) they were immediately labelled copies of Leone's movies. This assumption was further compounded by the similarity of Morricone's music in each film, which often sounded very 'Dollar-esque.'

Similarly, it was assumed that composers working on Italian Westerns were influenced by Morricone's style. But more often than not they produced material that bore little resemblance to Morricone's music and was original in its own right. Luis Bacalov's dark, gloomy score to *Django* could never be mistaken for Morricone. The same goes for Riz Ortolani's breezy, brassy title music to *Day Of Anger*. Among the best of the other composers are Gianni Ferrio, Nico Fidenco and Bruno Nicolai. Roberto Pregadio has the honour of composing one of the most familiar pieces of Spaghetti Western music, though few people actually know what it's called, where it comes from or who wrote it. This haunting whistled theme, which appears whenever a suitable Spaghetti Western atmosphere is required (in anything from adverts to holiday programmes), is the theme from *Gunmen Of Ave Maria* (1970) also rather aptly known as *The Forgotten Pistolero*. This piece is a formula composition, the classic example of a Morricone pastiche. Morricone's style was later parodied by Marcello Giombini (with *Sabata*), Franco Micalizzi (*They Call Me Trinity*) and Guido and Maurizio De Angelis (who came into their own in the seventies with scores including *Trinity Is Still My Name* and *Keoma*), when Spaghettis themselves moved into more light-hearted territory. Even Morricone eventually adapted his style at the end of the Spaghetti boom and ended up parodying himself.

The key collaborator throughout the Western cycle was Alessandro Alessandroni, an immensely important figure, who worked with most of the main composers on many of the finest Westerns. His distinctive whistling and guitar playing, and the diverse vocal talents of his choir are instantly recognisable. Never more so than in *The Good, The Bad And The Ugly* - Morricone's most famous score - where bizarre shrieks and whoops replace the whistled melodies of the previous two *Dollars* films. Morricone was experimenting with using human voices to replicate animalistic sounds - the howl of a coyote, the screech of a bird - and this is most apparent on the raw vocals used in *The Good, The Bad And The Ugly* and other films of the period like *The Hills Run Red* and *Navajo Joe*. The howls in *The Good, The Bad And The Ugly* were applied like signature tunes to each of the three main characters, and freeze-frames and title cards introduced each of the main characters ('the ugly', 'the bad' and 'the good' respectively) as the film progressed, though even this title card device was borrowed from the American B-Western *Rage At Dawn* (1955), where they introduced the villainous Reno brothers. But *The Good, The Bad And The Ugly* also featured the soprano vocals of Edda Del'Orso, a pure, ethereal voice that would become synonymous with Morricone's best scores. In *The Good, The Bad And The Ugly*, she performs Morricone's pounding 'Ecstasy Of Gold' theme that accompanies Tuco's search for the $200,000 grave at the film's climax. Del'Orso's voice was used to even greater effect on 'Jill's Theme' from *Once Upon A Time In The West*, one of Morricone's most moving compositions. In fact Leone and Morricone's relationship was such that the themes for *Once Upon A Time* were written before Leone started shooting. The film also featured the track 'Man With A Harmonica', which was the ultimate version of Morricone's gundown themes up to that point.

For all the competition, Morricone was the foremost composer of the genre. Morricone's scores often made the films successful, while even some of the worst Westerns are bearable, if only to hear his accompaniments. His scoring was sometimes formulaic, and his pieces were often reused from film to film, but they were far away from the epic, brassy (and sometimes interminably slow) scores from American Westerns. He also quoted liberally from classical music, stealing phrases, passages and whole compositions (which he re-orchestrated) from Mozart, Beethoven, Mussorgsky and Wagner. If Spaghetti Western music conformed to a loose formula, it would read thus: Spaghetti title themes are usually up-tempo, catchy and anarchic, and are often accompanied by cartoonish, pop-art title sequences featuring action and stills from the film. Moments of tension tend to be scored with unsettling atonal sound effects, mingled with the clever use of actual sounds (horses hooves, spurs, the wind, a creaking sign). Gunfights are preceded by extended scenes where the protagonists stare at each other, waiting to draw, while triumphal trumpets, church organs and guitars whip up a macabre bolero before the moment of death. Pathos is added to other scenes with elegiac, delicate melodies - themes that seem a million miles from the violent world conveyed on screen. *Navajo Joe* (1966) wouldn't be as effective without Morricone's wailing, electrified take on Native American Indian music. The chase through the cane fields in *The Big Gundown* (1966) would be less than impressive with anything other than Morricone's percussion-driven tour de force, and the mute gunslinger's bloody death in *The Big Silence* (1967) wouldn't pack such a punch without Morricone's plaintive reprise of the 'Love Theme'. Moreover, *The Good, The Bad And The Ugly* and *Once Upon A Time In The West* are almost totally reliant on music to make their visuals, plot twists, action sequences and humour successful.

By the late sixties, Morricone was becoming a major force in the Italian film industry. Apart from working on dozens of Westerns (35 in all), he worked on both award-winning art cinema projects and genre trash, ignoring snobbishness and creating effective, apt scores for both camps. On the arty side, he provided music for critically acclaimed movies like Marco Bellocchio's *Fists In The Pocket* (1965), Gillo Pontecorvo's *The Battle Of Algiers* (1966) and *Burn* (1969), Pier Paolo Pasolini's *Hawks And Sparrows* and *Theorem* (1968), Bernardo Bertolucci's *1900* (1977) and Elio Petri's *Investigation Of A Citizen Above Suspicion* (1969). At the other end of the spectrum, Morricone worked on most of the popular Cinecittà genres of the sixties and early seventies. From black and white Gothic Horrors (*Night Of The Doomed*), Spy movies (*Operation Bloody Mary* and *Matchless*), Sci-Fi (*Danger: Diabolik*), War Movies (*The Dirty Heroes*), Thrillers (*Wake Up And Kill, Grand Slam* and *The Sicilian Clan*), Adventures (*The Rover* and *The Red Tent*) and Giallo Horrors (*The Bird With The Crystal Plumage*). His prolific output and obvious talent resulted in his transition to Hollywood movies in the seventies, though the results (on movies like *Exorcist II* and *Orca - Killer Whale*) were often indifferent. One of his most famous pieces of the eighties was 'Chi Mai' (initially written for *Maddalena* a decade earlier) which was used by the BBC TV series *The Life And Times Of David Lloyd George* and became a hit. But it was his involvement in Leone's last film *Once Upon A Time In America* (1984) and *The Mission* (1986) that revitalised his career and finally announced to the world that Morricone was one of the most important film composers of the twentieth century. Initially, Morricone refused to work on *The Mission*, but not because of money. Having seen a rough cut, he felt the film was so powerful that he couldn't do the images justice, though he was eventually persuaded otherwise.

Morricone has been nominated for an Oscar four times (*Days Of Heaven*, *The Mission*, *The Untouchables* and *Bugsy*) but never won, which is incredible considering his oeuvre. The most enduring aspect of his scores, be they Westerns or otherwise, is their listenability. Morricone is one of the most collected soundtrack composers in the world, with each successive generation of film fans entranced by his genius with a melody. He has even taken to conducting his scores live, as in the celebrated concert at Santa Cecilia in 1998. Even years later, their power is undiminished, as *The Mission* and *Cinema Paradiso* sit beside *The Good, The Bad And The Ugly* and *Burn*. This is especially noticeable in the exquisite choral arrangements and solo vocalists. It is also strange how stars like Eastwood have become synonymous with Morricone's music. Though the actor has only appeared in a few films scored by Morricone since his Spaghetti jaunt (*The Witches*, *Two Mules For Sister Sara* and *In The Line Of Fire*), most Eastwood documentaries make liberal use of Morricone on the soundtrack, even in the sections of his life not dealing with his Italian work. And when the American Film Institute honoured Eastwood for services to the industry, he arrived at the gala to the stirring strains of 'Ecstasy Of Gold' from *The Good, The Bad And The Ugly*, reiterating how important Leone's films were to his career. Ironically, though Morricone now composes for Hollywood blockbusters, writes cantatas and has received great critical acclaim, the mere mention of his name still conjures up his Westerns, and images of dusty landscapes and ruthless gunslingers.

Rome On The Range: 1964-65

A Fistful Of Dollars (1964)

Director Sergio Leone

Cast: Clint Eastwood (The Stranger), Gian Maria Volonte (Ramon Rojo), Marianne Koch (Marisol) 97 minutes

Story: Into the small Mexican town of San Miguel rides a poncho-clad gunslinger. The town is run by two rival gangs - a group of American gun-runners called the Baxters, and the Rojos, a bunch of Mexican liquor smugglers, led by Ramon. The stranger becomes a hired gun for the Rojos to escalate the conflict, but he later sees the Mexicans steal a shipment of army gold from the Federales. He cleverly plays one side off against the other, and is paid for his services, whilst saving the lives of a Mexican woman Marisol and her family. But his ruse is discovered by the Rojos, who capture and beat him up. He escapes and the Mexicans presume he has sheltered with the Baxters. In a ruthless attack, the Rojos burn down the Baxters' house and massacre the entire clan, but the stranger has already left town. He recovers in hiding and returns to town to face the Rojos. In the showdown, he defeats the gang (using a square piece of iron hidden beneath his poncho as a breastplate), kills Ramon in a duel and rides out of town with a fistful of dollars.

Background: Leone's first Western is the foundation stone of the entire Spaghetti Western concept. Moreover, with *The Magnificent Seven* (1960) it is the most important Western of the sixties. It is ironic that such a defining film was made the same year that the greatest Western director of all time, John Ford, made his last Western, *Cheyenne Autumn*, which to some extent apologised for the mistreatment of Indians by film-makers down the years. *A Fistful Of Dollars* was a million miles away from Ford's vision of the West, created an international megastar and kick-started an entire genre under the most extraordinary of circumstances. Looking to remake Akira Kurosawa's Samurai movie *Yojimbo* (1961), Leone (using the pseudonym Bob Robertson) and his writers (including an uncredited Duccio Tessari) reworked the Japanese sword-flick as a Western - just as *The Magnificent Seven* had its roots in Kurosawa's *Seven Samurai* (1954). Leone even called his version 'The Magnificent Stranger'. But both *Yojimbo* and *A Fistful Of Dollars* owe a debt to crime writer Dashiell Hammett, who penned similar town-feud scenarios in *Red Harvest* and the clever Western whodunnit *Corkscrew*. For the role of the hero originally played by Toshiro Mifune, Leone approached two of the 'Seven', Charles

Bronson and James Coburn, and also Henry Fonda. After failing to goad any of them across the Atlantic, Leone eventually hired American TV actor Clint Eastwood, who was playing Rowdy Yates in *Rawhide*. On Eastwood's arrival in Rome, Leone completely overhauled his clean-cut image, as the production began shooting, first in Cinecittà Studios in Rome and later on location in the deserts and mountains of Almeria, Southern Spain.

Dressed in a Mexican poncho, with a couple of days stubble and a cigar held tightly between his teeth, Eastwood ushered in a new style of anti-hero. Steve McQueen and James Coburn had already experimented with the 'strong silent type' in Westerns, but under Leone's direction, Eastwood's vocal performance was pared to a minimum. The original script was very long-winded and Eastwood cut dialogue at every opportunity. He even had the first of the many quirky catchphrases of his career, when he utters in the final duel: "When a man with a .45 meets a man with a rifle, you said the man with the pistol's a dead man. Let's see if that's true." It's not, incidentally. When the film was released in America, the adverts dubbed Eastwood 'The Man With No Name', though it was really only a marketing ploy by United Artists. It is important that both Leone and Eastwood claimed to have created this new Western anti-hero. In actual fact, neither could have done it without the others' participation. Leone's vision plus Eastwood's image resulted in an astoundingly fresh approach to the old myths.

But everything about *A Fistful Of Dollars* (as Leone's film would be rechristened) was refreshing and different, from the harsh desert landscape, the brutal censor-defying violence, the imaginative music and the exotic, suntanned cast. The international co-production employed performers from Italy and Germany in the other main roles with the rest made up of Spaniards (both professional actors and assorted locals and wranglers who lived in Almeria). The music was a major contributing factor to the film and nothing like it had been heard before. Working in collaboration with Leone, Ennio Morricone and his whistling, guitar-playing associate Alessandro Alessandroni breathed new life into Western scoring, producing something akin to a Western pop song, which absorbed elements from classical music, folk music, beat music and opera.

A Fistful Of Dollars is a fast paced, beautifully photographed action movie. The San Miguel town set was used many times, before and since, but never to such excellent effect. And the atmosphere Leone creates is unique from the off - the stranger's meeting with four toughs at the beginning of the movie has passed into history. They scare his mule with gunshots and he strides to face them, pausing to order three coffins from the local undertaker. He provokes the gunmen with almost parodic dialogue - "My mule don't like people laughing. Gets the crazy idea your laughing at him" - before flicking back his poncho and gunning them down in double-quick time. As he nonchalantly walks back down the street he adds to the undertaker, "My mistake, four coffins." Never had violence in a Western been so fast, seemed so appealing and looked as cool. Critics loathed lumbering, emotionless Eastwood and his swarthy adversaries, but audiences knew better. One snooty critic complained that the dubbed voices all employed the same brand of 'Mexican mummerset', that the Technicolor process gave the film a 'pulmonary flush' and that the action sequences looked 'as though tomato sauce had been sloshed over a rather wretched meal.' Audiences didn't care - they probably thought a pulmonary flush was a type of toilet. 97 action-packed minutes turned Eastwood into *the* Western anti-hero of the sixties. As the posters claimed: 'He's going to trigger a whole new style of adventure.' And he did - the world over.

The Verdict: Reinvention doesn't really cover what Leone and Eastwood did in 1964, but the film's huge and enduring success is a testament to their achievement on a very low budget - even more so when you realise neither could speak the other's language. When a director with imagination meets an actor with star potential, the man taking the money's going to clean up. 4/5

One Silver Dollar (1964)

Director Giorgio Ferroni

Cast: Giuliano Gemma (Gary O'Hara), Ida Galli (Judy O'Hara), Pierre Cressoy (McCory) 88 minutes

Story: At the end of the Civil War, two Confederate brothers, Gary and Phil O'Hara, separate - Gary goes home to his wife, while Phil heads West. Bored by life in peacetime Richmond, Gary soon follows Phil. Gary is hired by a wealthy banker, McCory, to kill a local outlaw, Blacky, but the outlaw is actually Phil and the two brothers are ambushed. Phil dies, but Gary survives and sets about defeating the banker, who is in league with a bunch of renegades masquerading as Confederate raiders. Eventually it transpires that Phil was innocent, that McCory is the real villain (foreclosing on the local farmers' debts) and the local Sheriff is also involved, so Gary sets the record straight.

Background: This was the first of a trilogy of Westerns Gemma made with Ferroni between 1964 and 1967. The only consistent features are the presence of Gemma (in each film playing a character with the Christian name Gary), director Ferroni (as 'Calvin Jackson Padget') and some of the supporting cast and crew (including composer Gianni Ferrio). Like the Ringo films (also starring Gemma), this trilogy, and in particular *One Silver Dollar*, harks back to fifties American series Westerns, with an added dose of violence. *One Silver Dollar* was followed by the best of the trio, *Fort Yuma Gold* (1966), an extremely entertaining Civil War-set Spaghetti that has a similar atmosphere (roving bands of guerrillas, ruined towns) to Leone's *The Good, The Bad And The Ugly*, though obviously on a lower budget. Here Gary Hammond (Gemma) must deliver a warning despatch to Union Fort Yuma (a gold reserve), before a gang of renegade Confederates infiltrate the stockade. That was followed by *Wanted* (1967), a more pedestrian tale of a Sheriff, Gary Ryan (Gemma), trying to expose a counterfeit branding ring. All three feature a strong central relationship between Gemma and a girl. Female characterisation was never a great strength of Spaghettis, but these films (especially the first two) make a commendable effort. Many didn't bother with women and those that did made a pretty poor job of depicting them with anything more than cardboard conviction - epitomised by Gemma's love interest in *Fort Yuma Gold*, a dance-hall girl named Connie Breastfull.

Gemma's character is always a good man, forced through circumstance to become responsible for other people's lives. In two of the films he must clear his own blackened name, in the other embark on a mission that will save hundreds of lives. Gemma, like in his Ringo films, is an appealing hero and the excellent villains (Cressoy, ex-muscleman Dan Vadis or Serge Marquand) and the imaginative music (by Gianni Ferrio, sometimes in collaboration with Morricone or Alessandroni) ensure that the series was more interesting that more run-of-the-mill Spaghettis. *One Silver Dollar* is so called because the scriptwriters used the old chestnut of the hero's life being saved by a lucky coin in his breast pocket. The one aspect Ferroni did borrow from Leone however was the fact that the hero got tortured at some point in the movie (in *Yuma* he's even periodically blinded) making his vengeance all the more sweet.

The Verdict: One Silver Dollar was praised in Italy for its realistic depiction of the post-Civil War South (which in the movie is as cliché-ridden as any Hollywood attempt, complete with southern belle and Negro mammy), but it set Gemma up nicely for the first Ringo film, *A Pistol For Ringo*, which appeared the following year. 2/5 for *Silver*, 3/5 for *Yuma* and 2/5 for *Wanted*, the least interesting of the series.

Seven Guns For The MacGregors (1965)

Director Franco Giraldi

Cast: Robert Woods (Gregor MacGregor), Leo Anchoriz (Santillana), Fernando Sancho (Miguel), Agatha Flory (Rosita) 92 minutes

Story: A family of Scottish horse ranchers live with their seven sons on their secluded homestead. When the sons take their horses to market, they have them stolen by a gang of Mexican bandits in league with a local sheriff. The sons set off to try to recover the herd and Gregor (the cleverest of the brothers) infiltrates a Mexican gang, led by Santillana. Gregor dupes the bandits out of some gold, but they capture him and his girl Rosita. She tells Santillana where the brothers and the gold are hiding, but Gregor manages to save his siblings just as they are about to be executed. The bandits surround them and all seems lost, until Rosita arrives with a rescue party, who save the day and rout the bandits, leaving the MacGregors rich.

Background: This is the first successful comedy Spaghetti and the best Italian Western directed by Franco Giraldi (who also used the pseudonym Frank Grafield). Giraldi was Leone's assistant director on *A Fistful Of Dollars*, while one of the scriptwriters on *Seven Guns For The MacGregors* was the talented Duccio Tessari. The violence of Giraldi's film recalls some of the more brutal moments of *A Fistful Of Dollars*, but the humorous narrative, parodic performances and slapstick fist fights lighten the mood. At one point a gringo is dragged alive through a fire, but the moment of horror is offset by the Mexican torturer moaning that gringos are 'much too soft.' A more interesting plot twist was when Gregor joins Santillana's band (like Eastwood in *For A Few Dollars More*), but instead of gunning down the gang, he tips his brothers off about the bandits' forthcoming robberies (a bank, a gold convoy, a train shipment). When the bandits (led by Santillana's incompetent lieutenant Miguel) arrive, the MacGregors have got there first and relieved the safes of their contents. These and other scenes strongly resemble Tessari's Ringo films (in particular *A Pistol For Ringo*), where stock characters and situations are expertly lampooned. Robert Woods is an excellent easygoing hero, though he, like the other six badly-dubbed brothers, doesn't bother attempting a Scottish accent. The stunt work's great, Morricone's Scottish pastiche score excellent (with drums, bagpipes and chants of 'Whisky and Glory! Hurrah for the MacGregors!') and Giraldi's direction keeps the action tripping along. Leo Anchoriz as the intimidating villain ends up dying during an exciting knife fight with Gregor on a waterwheel.

Following its success, Giraldi made a sequel called *Seven Women For The MacGregors* (1966), retitled *Up The MacGregors* for American distribution, with the same cast, except that American TV actor David Bailey took over the role of Gregor. The plot has the cache of gold from the first film stolen by another bunch of bandits, again led by Anchoriz (this time called Maldonado). More interestingly, the sons team up with a gang of Irish girls in an echo of *Seven Brides For Seven Brothers* (1954), with the Michael Kidd-choreographed dance numbers replaced by fisticuffs and gunplay. The film was again a cross between broad comedy (with plenty of rumbustious punch-ups between the Scots and the Irish over who has the best Whisky) and less than humorous violence, and had the dubious distinction of being released in America before *Seven Guns For The MacGregors* - quite possibly the only instance a sequel has beaten its predecessor to the cinema.

The Verdict: In common with the Ringo films and many early Spaghettis, *Seven Guns For The MacGregors* is nothing like Eastwood's Italian Westerns, but nevertheless it's a good laugh - particularly the opening scene, where the brothers' four elderly relatives foil an attack by a vicious but inept bandit gang. 3/5 each.

A Pistol For Ringo (1965)

Director Duccio Tessari

Cast: Giuliano Gemma (Ringo), Fernando Sancho (Sancho), Lorella De Luca (Miss Ruby), George Martin (Sheriff) 92 minutes

Story: The day before Christmas Eve in the town of Quemado, a Mexican bandit named Sancho and his gang rob the local bank. The Sheriff's posse give chase and Sancho is wounded, so the bandits hole up in a nearby ranch house, taking the occupants prisoner. Amongst the hostages are the owner Major Clyde and his daughter, Ruby (who is engaged to the Sheriff). Sancho will kill two captives a day until they are allowed to leave. The posse lay siege to the ranch and enlist the help of a young adventurer, named Ringo, who is currently locked in jail. He agrees to help, if he can have a percentage of the stolen money. He infiltrates the ranch, befriends Sancho and convinces the bandit that he's on their side. As the days pass Miss Ruby, though initially wary of Ringo's cockiness, falls for him. In a botched escape attempt, sabotaged by Ringo, the captives get away and Ringo faces the bandits, whom he manages to kill. By the time the posse and Ruby ride in, Ringo has taken his percentage and ridden into the sunset.

Background: After contributing to scripts for Leone (*A Fistful Of Dollars*) and Franco Giraldi (*Seven Guns For The MacGregors*), Tessari made a Western of his own in 1965. In place of the more contemporary, modernist style of Leone, Tessari approached *A Pistol For Ringo* in the classic Hollywood manner. Firstly he took a character name from American history (Johnny Ringo was a real gunfighter) which had already become a familiar name from Hollywood Westerns - John Wayne's character in John Ford's *Stagecoach* (1939) was named the Ringo Kid. For his Ringo Tessari cast up-and-coming leading man Giuliano Gemma, though Ringo is a far cry from Eastwood's ambivalent stranger. He is referred to throughout the film by the nickname Angel Face and he resembles conventional Hollywood heroes. He has principles, doesn't drink alcohol (preferring milk), but is still outside the law - he begins the film languishing in jail for gunning down four vengeful brothers (in self-defence, of course).

A Pistol For Ringo is a melding of the familiar and the ground-breaking. Ringo, the Sheriff and Miss Ruby are very Hollywood characters. The Sheriff (uniquely for Spaghettis) is honest and moral. In most efforts he would be in league with the bandits or too lethargic to intervene. Miss Ruby, the Sheriff's pretty fiancée (and in reality Tessari's wife) is also a stereotype, as she gradually falls for Ringo. Tessari's trick is to have these 'types' behave in unexpected ways, upsetting the expectations of traditional Westerns. The Mexican villains are more recognisably Italian in origin. Fernando Sancho's portrayal of a swaggering, moustachioed bandido is a true archetype for the Spaghettis that followed and guaranteed him work for years to come, though he was constantly typecast. By contrast, Sancho's señorita, a rough-and-ready bandita, changes during her stay at the hacienda and is finally civilised by the bourgeois ranch owner. The scruffy bandits dining in luxury make for some great comic situations.

The film is unusual in the Spaghetti Western canon, as it is set within a definite time period (the days leading up to Christmas), with the final escape attempt taking place on Christmas Day. A religious subtext even has Ringo waking up in a stable on Christmas Morning. The film is tightly plotted and surprisingly low on violence (barring the executions of the hostages), though it was still trimmed for foreign release - including a humorous scene where the bandits join in with the family carol singing. Ennio Morricone's score is inventive (even incorporating themes based on Silent Night), whilst still owing something to its Hollywood model. This is further echoed in the opening ballad 'Angel Face' - 'Ringo had an angel face, but whenever Ringo loved, Ringo fought.' The film was unexpectedly successful in America in 1966 (where its release predated the arrival of the Dollars films in 1967), probably because audiences appreciated

Tessari's knowing exploitation of the genre's conventions. Plus it also looked like one of the more imaginative American B-Westerns of the fifties because of a more youthful, appealing cast (Italian Gemma hid behind the hip pseudonym Montgomery Wood). If you're expecting a Leone-esque shoot-em-up, you'll be disappointed.

The Verdict: An excellent, well thought out little film that spawned several in-name-only sequels. Search out the only official follow-up - Tessari's own aptly titled *The Return Of Ringo*. 4/5

For A Few Dollars More (1965)

Director Sergio Leone

Cast: Clint Eastwood (Manco), Lee Van Cleef (Colonel Mortimer), Gian Maria Volonte (El Indio), Klaus Kinski (Hunchback) 125 minutes

Story: In the American Southwest, El Indio, a notorious Mexican bandit, is sprung from the Territorial Prison by his gang. With Indio on the loose, his reward reaches $10,000 dead or alive and two gringo bounty hunters decide to track him down. One is an ex-Confederate Colonel named Mortimer, while the other is Manco, a poncho-clad loner. Individually the pair figure out that Indio will try to rob the most impregnable vault in the territory at El Paso and arrive there to stake out the bank. Realising that they're after the same prey, the two finally team up and as part of their plan Manco infiltrates the bandit gang. But their scheme backfires and during the robbery Indio and his men get away with the safe and hide out in a Mexican village. Manco double-crosses Mortimer and rejoins the gang, but the Colonel shows up and offers to help Indio open the safe without damaging the contents. By night, the gringos manage to hide the loot, but they're caught and beaten. Indio releases them, so he can escape with the loot. The bandits are wiped out in a gunbattle and in the final showdown Mortimer kills Indio, settling an old vendetta with the bandit over the rape of Mortimer's sister. Manco is ready to split the $67,000 reward, but Mortimer allows his partner to keep it all - all he wanted was revenge.

Background: Eastwood and Leone's second film together established Eastwood's bankability and Leone's reputation as Italy's foremost action director. Even today *For A Few Dollars More* has lost none of its edge and hasn't dated at all. Eastwood, still in his poncho and chewing on a cigar, is this time a bounty hunter, giving a more interesting slant to the character from *A Fistful Of Dollars* (where he was a hired gun). Though even when Leone was exalting the importance of dollars over life itself, Eastwood's partner, Van Cleef's Colonel Mortimer, introduced the idea of conscience, absolution and revenge. But it was the villain, again played by Volonte, that really pushed the genre to pastures new. With Eastwood and Van Cleef as grim-faced, passionless killers (the ultimate in stylish gunslingers), Volonte, as a drug-addicted, religion-fixated rapist was the most excessive character to appear in a Western up to 1965. In fact, few since have equalled his over-the-top sadism and egotistic obsessiveness. Drugs had never appeared in mainstream Westerns and sexual assault was something that happened off-screen (and then only hinted at). It certainly wasn't depicted as a red-tinted reverie as it is here. This, the sparse female characterisations (if mere walk-ons can be termed as such) and the macho emphasis on violence (especially a scene where Indio's whole gang interminably beat up the two gringos) led to the film being written off as savage, misogynistic trash - acceptable in Italy, but definitely not in America, the historical heartland of the Western. Ironic then that *For A Few Dollars More* made a fortune when finally released there in July 1967.

To many, this is Leone's finest Western and it certainly epitomises everything Spaghettis were best at. Greed and revenge, violence and betrayal, gringos versus Mexican bandidos, bank robberies, evocative music and protracted duels. When Mortimer faces Indio in the finale, in a makeshift circular Roman arena, Leone stretched the moment before the draw to breaking point. Ennio Morricone's triumphant trumpet theme spiralled skywards and then cut to silence, as the tight-lipped protagonists let their guns do the talking. Having made Eastwood a star (and seemingly quickly tiring of his new cinematic creation) Leone added a second hero, who effectively became the lead. For the Colonel, Leone again looked to America. After being snubbed by Henry Fonda, Charles Bronson and Lee Marvin, he cast hawk-nosed Van Cleef (a Hollywood villain from *High Noon*, *Gunfight At The OK Corral* and *Ride Lonesome*). Volonte was again cast as the villain-in-chief and German actor Klaus Kinski appeared as a snarling, twitching hunchback (who in one scene has a match lit on his hump by Van Cleef).

The film was a fair improvement on *A Fistful Of Dollars*. The action sequences were punchier, the gringos were almost silent, their opponents (and the rest of the supporting cast) garrulous and operatic. Morricone's music was a considerable step forward, incorporating a twanging Jew's harp, eerie whistling, electric guitar and what sounds like someone levering a Winchester - and that was just the title tune. A plot device (a musical pocket watch) was also effortlessly woven in, making this one of Morricone's most intricate scores. After this movie, virtually every Spaghetti Western featured an extended, musical, montage-driven duel at the climax. And as if that wasn't innovative enough, Van Cleef had a pistol with a 12-inch barrel, a Derringer hidden up his sleeve and an arsenal of pistols and rifles hidden in his horse's blanket roll, which later influenced the gadget-led Sabata movies. A truly innovative movie and Eastwood got richer.

The Verdict: The untrustworthy partnership between the bounty hunter heroes has never been bettered, the Almerian landscapes never looked so beautiful and the Italian Western was never the same again. 5/5

The Return Of Ringo (1965)

Director Duccio Tessari

Cast: Giuliano Gemma (Ringo), George Martin (Paco), Fernando Sancho (Esteban), Lorella De Luca (Hally) 94 minutes

Story: Following the Civil War, a young Union Captain called Montgomery Brown (known as 'Ringo' to his friends) returns to his home town of Mimbres. He finds that a group of Mexican bandits - led by brothers Paco and Esteban Fuentes - have taken over the town and the Sheriff is powerless to stop the injustice. Ringo also finds out that Paco has designs on his wife Hally and the Mexicans are responsible for his father's death. The Mexicans are living in Ringo's house and have his wife and daughter prisoner. Paco plans to marry Hally and pretends that Ringo has been killed in battle. Ringo disguises himself as a Mexican peasant, goes into town and shelters in the house of a florist named Morning Glory. Eventually Ringo infiltrates the house and contacts his wife, but is captured and has his gun-hand crippled by Paco. Plotting revenge, he gathers a small group of allies, including the florist, an Indian medicine man and the cowardly drunken Sheriff. Threatening Hally that her daughter will be harmed, Paco convinces her to marry him. But during the ceremony, Ringo returns - not in his beggars rags, but in his true guise, his Cavalry uniform. While a dust storm rages, Ringo and his accomplices rout Paco and the Mexicans, and save his wife and daughter.

Background: Notoriously economical when it came to deploying their resources, the Italian film industry flourished by reusing sets, costumes and actors (not to mention plots) throughout any given 'genre explosion.' *The Return Of Ringo* epitomises this. It was made by the same director and production team responsible for the first Ringo film (*A Pistol For Ringo*) with the same cast and locations. But to give the impression that the sequel is far removed from *Pistol*, they all play different characters (for example, George Martin plays the villainous Paco rather than the Sheriff). All except Giuliano Gemma, who reprises his role as the young hero Ringo. Even then, his characterisation is only vaguely related to the original Ringo - instead of a young outlaw, he's a cavalry captain returning from the Civil War. This time Tessari is more specific with his reference points. There are allusions to Howard Hawks' Westerns (in particular *Rio Bravo*, with its drunken Sheriff and ragtag bunch of misfits facing tyranny) and Ringo's ride through the desert at the film's opening recalls John Ford's cavalry movies, but Tessari's sources go back a lot further than the late forties. *The Return Of Ringo* is basically a rewrite of Homer's *The Odyssey*, the mythical story of Odysseus' voyage home after the Trojan War. For Odysseus read Ringo, for Penelope read Hally. Paco Fuentes and his gang represent the suitors, jostling for Penelope's hand. The Trojan War may have become the Civil War, but Tessari intelligently Westernises the story, creating a film of power and complexity.

Not only that, Tessari cleverly parodied *A Fistful Of Dollars*, the most popular Spaghetti schema of the time - the irony being that to everyone in town, Ringo (disguised as a beggar) is a stranger in town, when in reality he's a local. Only at the end, on Paco and Hally's wedding day, does Ringo reveal his true identity. In the most impressive scene in the film (based on an image from *The Odyssey*) Ringo appears framed in the church doorway in a swirling sandstorm. Instead of his beggars rags, he's now wearing his cavalry uniform and Paco is totally unnerved.

With its foundations in Classic Westerns and Classical mythology, Tessari added some decidedly odd characters to the melting-pot. These include changing Odysseus' son into a cherubic, blonde (and quite frankly irritating) daughter and incorporating two genre firsts - a fortune-telling whore and a camp florist named Morning Glory (who eventually gets fed up with making funeral wreaths and joins Ringo). Ennio Morricone's score, like *A Pistol For Ringo*, verges on the traditional (it again features a wholesome ballad) and also includes references to classical compositions. In the Italian print of the movie, Morning Glory is called 'Myosotis' (a reference to the flower 'Forget-Me-Not'), a more apt name considering that Ringo returns home to a town that has forgotten him. It's a clever gag that is completely lost in translation.

The Verdict: Without reaching the dizzying heights of Leone and Corbucci, Tessari made an important contribution to the genre with this movie. His films were less about stretching the boundaries of the Western and more about ironic homages to the genre's giants, though what John Ford would have thought of this movie is open to debate. Even so, this is Tessari's best film and one of the most intelligent, thought-provoking Italian Westerns. 4/5

Coffers Full Of Dollars: 1966

A Bullet For The General (1966)

Director Damiano Damiani

Cast: Gian Maria Volonte (El Chuncho), Klaus Kinski (Santo), Lou Castel (Tate), Martine Beswick (Adelita) 114 minutes

Story: During the Mexican Revolution, a young gringo called Tate joins a band of Mexican gun-runners working for the revolutionaries. The band is led by Chuncho (who's in it for the money) and his half-brother Santo (a believer in the cause). They steal guns from the government to sell to General Elias, whose hideout is in the hills. On the way, the gang stop off at San Miguel and help the peasants kill their rich, exploitative boss. But after their liberation, they want Chuncho to stay on as mayor. Chuncho seems keen, but Tate is determined to get to Elias and convinces the rest of the gang to leave with the guns. Eventually Chuncho abandons Santo and the peasants and rejoins his gang, but in a battle with government troops, the gun-runners are decimated. Chuncho and Tate survive and continue alone to Elias' headquarters, though the Mexican has to nurse the gringo when he catches malaria. At the HQ, Chuncho sells the guns but General Elias sentences him to death - San Miguel has been attacked, the peasants massacred, but the armaments could have prevented it. Santo escapes and is about to kill Chuncho when Tate intervenes and kills Santo and Elias. Weeks later, Chuncho and Tate meet up in Cuidad Juarez and Tate tells him that he is a hired assassin and their whole relationship has been an elaborate ruse to complete his contract. With that, Chuncho shoots Tate as they are boarding a train to the US - the Mexican is no longer a bloodthirsty bandit, but a revolutionary.

Background: This is the only Spaghetti Western to successfully deal with the Mexican Revolution with anything remotely resembling incisiveness. Corbucci's imaginative political Westerns were much more light-hearted in their commitment, while other attempts, like *Tepepa* (1968), *Run Man Run* (1968) and Leone's *Duck You Sucker* (1971), either didn't have the power to convey the key issues of the Mexican people or got lost in star-leaden, overblown scenarios - films that existed purely to blow up trains, bridges and extras as elaborately as possible. Most forgot what the word revolution actually meant.

Damiani didn't and *A Bullet For The General*, based on an excellent screenplay by political writer Franco Solinas (*Salvatore Giuliano*, *The Battle Of Algiers*), was much more than a succession of over-the-top set pieces. Carefully constructed, the film featured plenty of action, but the story was a strong element in the film. The relationships between the main characters highlighted the differing perspectives of the revolution. Chuncho is a bandit, seeing the war as an opportunity to make a few pesos. Santo is a priest, devoutly observing his twin beliefs - God and the revolutionary people. Tate, a character who for much of the film seems quite sympathetic, is the ultimate betrayer (a government assassin) and Adelita is a peasant girl who rides with Chuncho's hombres, but finds that through the gringo's manipulation she has lost all that she holds dear (her lover, another of Chuncho's band). Along the way, this gang encounter various groups (the army, peasants, political prisoners and revolutionaries) and their presentation in the film is utterly convincing.

There are moments when it is obvious that this is a Spaghetti Western, like the golden bullet that Tate carries in his valise, that is accompanied by *The Good, The Bad And The Ugly*-type riff on the soundtrack - hammering home its significance to the story. But for the most part, Damiani has succeeded in his aim, which was to make a serious statement about the Mexican Revolution. Even the usually excessive Kinski is more subdued as the monastically-clad pistol-packing padre, though in one sequence he is allowed to indulge in histrionics and throw hand grenades at an army parade in the name of the 'Father, Son and Holy Ghost.' The film was originally called *El Chuncho - Quien Sabe?* ('El Chuncho - Who Knows?), an inquisitive title that is as elliptical as Solinas' plot.

The Verdict: This is much better than Castel's other Political Western, *Requiescant* (1967) directed by Carlo Lizzani. Damiani gets the balance right between tension, action, politics and history and allows his characters to develop. Not your usual Spaghetti then, but that was Damiani's intention. *Bullet* was a surprise commercial success and opened the floodgates for the Political Westerns that followed. 4/5

The Good, The Bad And The Ugly (1966)

Director Sergio Leone

Cast: Clint Eastwood (Blondy 'The Good'), Lee Van Cleef (Angel Eyes 'The Bad'), Eli Wallach (Tuco 'The Ugly'), Luigi Pistilli (Brother Pablo), Al Mulock (Bounty Hunter) 167 minutes

Story: During the Civil War, Angel Eyes, a hired gun, learns of a shipment of Confederate army gold that has vanished and sets about locating the one man who can identify its whereabouts, a Confederate cavalryman called Bill Carson. Meanwhile, a bounty hunter named Blondy has joined up with Tuco, a Mexican outlaw, in a bounty scam. But after Blondy double-crosses Tuco, the Mexican takes him into the desert to torture and kill him. There they encounter Carson, half-dead, who tells each of them one part of the gold's location. Tuco knows that the cache is buried in a War cemetery on Sad Hill, while Blondy learns the name on the specific grave. Now disguised as Confederate soldiers, Blondy recovers at a monastery functioning as a war hospital (run by Tuco's brother Pablo). Moving on, they are captured by a Union patrol and taken to a Yankee prison camp, where Angel Eyes is working as a Sergeant. He tortures the name of the cemetery out of Tuco and packs him off to jail, while Blondy sides with Angel Eyes and his gang to find the gold. Later Tuco (who has escaped his escort) and Blondy are reunited and wipe out Angel Eyes' gang, though their leader evades them. Continuing towards the graveyard, the duo intervene in a battle for a strategically important bridge, blowing it sky high. Eventually finding the vast cemetery, they also find Angel Eyes and the three shoot it out with a fortune at stake. Blondy kills Angel Eyes and outwits Tuco, takes half the money and rides into the distance, while Tuco is left alive - rich but without a horse.

Background: This is probably the most famous Spaghetti Western of them all, no doubt due to Ennio Morricone's distinctive theme tune (which everyone, whether they've seen the film or not, is familiar with). Moreover *The Good, The Bad And The Ugly* is one of the most popular, enduring Westerns ever. Along with *The Searchers, The Magnificent Seven, Once Upon A Time In The* West, *The Wild Bunch* and *Butch Cassidy And The Sundance Kid*, it is regularly voted into contemporary audiences' Top 100 films of all time (the kind of poll that has whatever is No.1 at the box office that week in the top spot). It is also unusual, in that it works not only as an action film, but also as a great art movie and a morality tale - seldom has a Western looked so beautiful and asked so many questions about human nature. It is truly epic in scale, even more so than Leone's next film, *Once Upon A Time In The West*, as the Blue and the Grey (actually the Spanish army in period costume) fight it out as the backdrop to Leone's treasure hunt.

Leone recast his two leading men from *For A Few Dollars More*, but altered their characters. Eastwood was now Blondy, more a cunning con-man than a bounty hunter, while Van Cleef was the villainous hired gun, christened 'Angel Eyes' (originally called Setenza in the Italian version, which means sentence, as in 'death sentence'). Eastwood even abandoned his trademark poncho for the film (he only wears it in the final gunfight, after he steals it from a dead Confederate). But Leone was obviously less concerned with Blondy and Angel Eyes and more interested in the character of garrulous, foul-mouthed Mexican bandido Tuco (played by Wallach, who appeared in *The Magnificent Seven*). For the first time in a Leone movie, we see a major character with their guard down. Tuco comes across as a slightly inept, bumbling outlaw and is easily outwitted and double-crossed by Blondy, but nevertheless, using his own distinctive methods he manages to survive. He is also a fall guy for Eastwood. It is Tuco who always ends up on his knees in the dust or dangling precariously from a rope, while Blondy strides through every situation without breaking sweat. For this humiliation and betrayal, Tuco leads Blondy into the wasteland to kill him (but inevitably fails). We also learn more about Tuco's character than was expected in a Leone film. In one affecting scene, he visits his brother (a monk) and learns of the death of his parents.

The intricacies of the plot are down to Leone, Luciano Vincenzoni and an uncredited Sergio Donati (who co-scripted Sergio Sollima's best movies and *Once Upon A Time In The West*). Like all the best adventure films (and *The Good, The Bad And The Ugly* is a period adventure film as much as a Western) it relies on outrageous coincidence and surprise to power the story and captivate the viewer. The initial premise upon which the whole story rests takes place before the film has even begun. A Union patrol ambush a Confederate gold shipment. Only three of the escort survive and one of them hides the cache in a grave. Only Angel Eyes does any detective work to locate the cache, Blondy and Tuco become involved in the search by chance, and the treasure hunt is only a small part of the movie. There are also some great lines of dialogue - "If you have to shoot, shoot...don't talk", "There are two kinds of people in the world my friend", "I always see my job through" and the logical, "Two can dig a lot quicker than one."

But it is the imaginative Civil War setting that allows Leone the opportunity to inject pathos into his West. The War gave him the chance to direct epic scenes and it must have amused him staging the battle sequences in Spain (a second Spanish Civil War). Every detail looks authentic (though several aren't) and the Civil War of *The Good, The Bad And The Ugly* is the most convincing cinematic staging of the conflict. Refugees flee ruined towns, generals are reduced to travelling on rickety wagons, armies are shifted by railroad and soldiers kill and loot (and are executed when they are caught). This was a violent, merciless war, based partly on WW1 (with entrenched armies fighting over a bridge at the behest of their idiot commanders) and WW2 (a prison camp with starving rag-clothed inmates, high fences, gravediggers and death wagons piled high with corpses). If this film had depicted either of those more contemporary conflicts, it would have run into serious censorship problems.

The Good, The Bad And The Ugly begins as a pretty standard Spaghetti Western (a shoot-out in a ghost town, a killing at a farm, a murder, a fumbled ambush) but the Civil War becomes more apparent as the film progresses and hangs over the action like a vulture. The first soldier who appears in the film is a legless Confederate reduced to selling information for a price, while several shots dwell on the dead or severely injured. The Good is saddened by the conflict (seeing it as a waste of human life), The Bad runs a racket in a prison camp (selling on inmates' possessions), while to the Ugly, a Mexican, the War means nothing and merely slows down his route to the graveyard.

To the annoyance of several (mostly American) critics, there was still no room for women in Leone's West. While other Italian Western directors expanded the Leone formula and included meaty roles for actresses (in particular Tessari, Corbucci and Sollima), Leone stuck to a male-orientated world. The only women in the movie were prostitutes, hoteliers, peasants or farmers' wives. Even then, they either had one scene or had their scenes cut. In fact there have been several versions of the film available, of varying lengths, though a definitive cut has never been assembled. Love scenes for Eastwood were exorcised from both *For A Few Dollars More* and *The Good, The Bad And The Ugly* and sex doesn't enter into the equation. In this macho, war-torn world there aren't even any nurses in the hospitals. And again violence was directed at women, a feature of the film that Van Cleef, for one, loathed.

Though it's best remembered for Morricone's title theme - with its screaming, yelping vocals, cavalry trumpets and Shadows-style guitar, powered along by a pounding drumbeat - the score is much more than an echoing coyote howl in the desert. The Civil War scenes are accompanied by a haunting choral piece ('Ballad Of A Soldier') and a more expansive trumpet-led composition - as when Angel Eyes visits a Confederate hospital in a scene only included in Italian prints (though the piece is still present on the soundtrack album). Blondy's ordeal in the desert has an epic (as in Biblical epic) score, while Tuco's breathless search for the grave in the cross-strewn vastness is accompanied by one of Morricone's best ever tunes, the towering 'Ecstasy of Gold.' While there are none of the extended, montage-driven gundowns throughout the film, Leone makes up for it in the finale, where the three protagonists face each other in the huge circular arena in the middle of the graveyard. Here, the action (such as it is) consists of the three men staring meanly at each other for nearly five minutes - half of which consists of them taking their places at points on the circle, before the contest can begin, all accompanied by Morricone's macabre bolero.

The most astonishing aspect of the film is the way Leone varies the film's tempo - long scenes of silence (with little action), fast shoot-outs, chases, gags, pathos - but never loses his momentum. The camerawork (by Tonino Delli Colli) is superb, the performances perfect, the locations breathtaking. And for all its attempts at social comment (however successful or apparent), *The Good, The Bad And The Ugly* is also one of the great action Westerns. Eastwood has never been involved in a better film (though he'd probably argue he has), Van Cleef has never been more villainous, Wallach so overly dramatic and expressive. Its phenomenal success also resulted in the usual bunch of rip-offs, from Enzo G Castellari's *Seven Winchesters For A Massacre* (1967), with a poncho-clad hero involved in a Civil War treasure hunt, to *The Handsome, The Ugly And The Cretinous* (1967) a scene-for-scene slapstick version of Leone's film.

The Verdict: Though many claim that the films that bookend *The Good, The Bad And The Ugly* in Leone's canon (the vengeful *For A Few Dollars More* and epic *Once Upon A Time In The West*) are his finest work, *The Good, The Bad And The Ugly* is Leone's best film, made by a director at his zenith, with a global superstar-in-waiting in the lead and a fantastical plot that is never short on surprises. 5/5

The Big Gundown (1966)

Director Sergio Sollima

Cast: Lee Van Cleef (Corbett), Tomas Milian (Cuchillo), Walter Barnes (Brokston), Nieves Navarro (Widow), Fernando Sancho (Captain Segura) 102 minutes

Story: Ex-lawman turned bounty hunter Jonathan Corbett is hired by rich Texan railroad tycoon Brokston to track down a Mexican renegade called Cuchillo Sanchez. Nicknamed Sanchez the Knife he has allegedly raped and murdered a 14-year-old white girl. Made an 'honorary deputy', Corbett pursues the Mexican across Texas, but his prey outwits him at every turn, hiding out with a group of Mormons and later at a ranch ruled by the whip of a sadomasochistic Widow. Cuchillo escapes into Mexico, sheltering at a monastery and eventually makes it back to his wife in his home town. Corbett tracks him there, but Cuchillo slips through his fingers again, whereupon Brokston, the Baron (his German sidekick) and Brokston's son-in-law arrive and recruit a posse of Mexican rancheros. They flush Cuchillo out of the sugar-cane fields and corner him in the desert. But in the final reckoning it transpires that the real murderer is Brokston's son-in-law - the manhunt had been an elaborate ruse to leave the Brokston name unblemished. In a duel, Cuchillo kills the real culprit, whilst Corbett guns down the Baron and Brokston. The posse, seeing justice done, disband. Corbett and Cuchillo go their separate ways, each having learnt that wealth and power count for more in the West than the law, but that sometimes the truth can prevail.

Background: The Big Gundown is one of the finest Spaghettis ever made, but unfortunately, like so many, it is only available in cruelly abridged versions (respectively 95 and 84 minutes). Both versions remove much of the early and middle sections of the chase, including editing the beautiful opening duel when Corbett nails three bank robbers. The original story was written by political scenarist Franco Solinas. In this version, the lawman (a younger man) ended up killing his aged quarry without realising the truth. Sollima reversed the character's ages and threw in some troubling subject matter (sadomasochism/paedophilia), which inevitably led to censorship problems - in the 85-minute version no reference is made to the young girl's rape. Sollima also changed the ending to Solinas' story (making it more upbeat) and cast Van Cleef as the lawman (hot on the heels of his success in *The Good, The Bad And The Ugly*) and Tomas Milian, a Cuban ex-pat, as his younger, wily adversary. The film also adds a touch of satire, with bounty hunter Corbett harbouring political ambitions as a senator.

The Big Gundown borrowed extensively from previous Westerns (Cuchillo's knife-throwing skill is straight out of *The Magnificent Seven*, the crooked railroad magnate is a B-Western standard) but reassembled them so as to seem totally original. Consequently, *The Big Gundown* is equal to Leone's films, but most Western fans have never even heard of it, let alone seen it. By contrasting the two protagonists (a believer in the law and a tearaway 'rebel without a cause'), Sollima was making subtle political observations without resorting to (a) setting his film in the Mexican Revolution or (b) getting bogged down in a chin-stroking political debate. The points being made, though simplistic (poor, exploited peasantry 'good', rich tycoon 'bad') are the same points that several more lauded political films made, whilst being far more entertaining. Poor Cuchillo is even despised by his own people. The Mexican rancheros that Brokston recruits are happy to catch the peon, as he was once a revolutionary who sided with Juarez in the Mexican Revolution.

Van Cleef and Milian give career-best performances, both eliciting a degree of humanity as good but duped characters. Other turns of note are

Nieves Navarro as the wicked Widow, who puts Cuchillo in a pen with a wild bull, Walter Barnes as the disingenuous Brokston, a man prepared to twist the law to protect his family (and a forthcoming land deal), and Fernando Sancho, usually cast as a swaggering bandit, here portraying a Mexican officer who hates Mexican peasants and interfering Americans with equal relish. Sollima also includes some very interesting characters. Look out for an ex-gunslinger turned monk who is christened 'Brother Smith and Wesson' by his brethren, and the German Baron, complete with monocle and no sense of humour, who has a specially designed quick-draw holster, reinforcing his credo of 'speed over accuracy.' But although these characters seem to be self-conscious attempts by Sollima to make his movie different from run-of-the-mill Spaghettis, the authenticity of the settings and costumes makes this one of the most convincing portrayals of the West on celluloid. Ennio Morricone's music (including the title song 'Run Man Run') is an absolute classic and is among his most popular scores. The final chase through the cane fields is one of the great Spaghetti Western set pieces, as the hounds are unleashed and Cuchillo runs for his life. After the heights of *The Big Gundown*, Sollima made a direct sequel with Milian called *Run Man Run* (1968), but without Van Cleef and a decent script, the movie sank.

The Verdict: As good as they get. Though a decent print is as difficult to track down as Cuchillo himself, it's well worth the effort. 5/5

Django (1966)

Director Sergio Corbucci

Cast: Franco Nero (Django), Loredana Nusciak (Maria), Eduardo Fajardo (Major Jackson), Jose Bodalo (General Rodriguez) 87 minutes

Story: A mysterious coffin-dragging stranger named Django arrives in a nameless, muddy town. He discovers that the area is controlled by two warring groups - a Mexican bandit gang, led by General Rodriguez and a band of red-hooded Confederate Klansmen, led by the fanatical Major Jackson. Django wants to kill Jackson (for killing his wife) and in a massed gun battle in the main street he takes a machine-gun out of his coffin and decimates the Klan. Jackson escapes across the frontier into Mexico, so Django enlists the help of Rodriguez to attack a Mexican Army outpost and steal a fortune in gold. Their raid succeeds, but the General won't divide the proceeds. Double-crossed, Django steals the money, but is captured by the bandits and tortured, while the gold ends up in a pool of quicksand. The Mexicans cripple Django by crushing his hands, but later the bandits are trapped by Jackson and massacred. In the finale, Django meets Jackson and his men in a desolate graveyard, near his wife's grave. Though his hands are smashed, he manages to fire his pistol and gun down his adversaries, in memory of his wife.

Background: Corbucci had made three Westerns between 1964 and 1966 - *Red Pastures* (1964, aka *Massacre At Canyon Grande*), *Minnesota Clay* (1964) and *Johnny Oro* (1966, retitled *Ringo And His Golden Pistol*), but they hadn't made the impact of Leone's *A Fistful Of Dollars*. *Django* changed all that. Not only was it as revisionist as Leone's movies, it was one of the most distinctive Westerns ever made and had a huge impact on the Spaghetti Western boom, which hitherto had been ripping off the Dollars and Ringo films. Even today it's a powerful (though admittedly low-budget) piece of comic-strip cinema and its value to modern action movies is reiterated in the fact that there's a print of it in the Museum of Modern Art in New York.

Set in a mud-strewn border town, *Django* took the *A Fistful Of Dollars* plot dynamic (one hero against two warring factions) and ideas from *For A Few Dollars More* (flashy weaponry and revenge) and twisted it into a magnificent blood-splattered anti-Western. The hero, played by Italian Franco Nero, looked like no other protagonist of the era. Dressed in a long coat and black hat, he could be a soldier (there are allusions to him fighting for the Union in the Civil War) but the fingerless gloves, scarf and most of all, the omnipresent coffin add a more macabre, gravedigger quality to his appearance. The most memorable aspect of the film is his machine-gun, hidden in the box, which he periodically whips out to riddle the bad guys. Without a doubt, this was a very long way from John Wayne.

Corbucci, like Leone, kept his character mysterious and enigmatic (just as well, considering the appalling dubbing, which is the film's major failing) and the film fairly rips along, never wasting a second of its 87 minutes - economical film-making at its best. It also drew in a huge number of sources. The hero's name comes from Django Reinhardt, the French gypsy jazzman, whose guitar-playing style was dictated when his hand was badly burnt in a fire. The film also had its roots in offbeat fifties B-Westerns, Japanese samurai films and Horror movies. The other characters from *A Fistful Of Dollars* were altered considerably by Corbucci. Instead of the amiable tavern keeper and the jovial undertaker, Corbucci populates his town with a gaggle of tawdry whores and a dwarf violin-playing bartender. Even more excessive were *Django*'s adversaries. In place of gun-runners and liquor merchants, *Django* faces a group of down-trodden, vicious Mexican revolutionaries (led by a malicious, self-proclaimed General) and a bunch of racist, cross-burning Ku Klux Klansmen sporting red hoods (led by an über-redneck ex-Confederate Major). The film, even more than *A Fistful Of Dollars*, is a succession of Pop-Art set pieces. Some are action-packed - Django mowing down the Klansmen in the muddy main street, an attack on a Mexican army fort with the bandits posing as prostitutes. Some are sadistic - the Mexican General cuts the Klan priest's ear off and makes him eat it, and Django has his hands mangled. Others are downright bizarre - whores indulge in a spot of mud-wrestling and the Major shoots peons as though they were clay pigeons. *Django* is unrelentingly brutal and pessimistic and for all Corbucci's claims that the film addresses political issues (the North/South confrontation, the Major's racism, the Mexicans lying low during the revolution), any message is buried up to its neck in blood and mud.

It's difficult to assess *Django*'s influence on American Westerns as the film was never formally released there or the UK, though Jack Nicholson did reportedly try to buy the rights in 1967. On the continent the film made Nero a superstar and began a whole sub-genre (trading on the Django name), which runs to about twenty movies - but far more if you count retitled cash-ins (mostly the German and French versions of completely unrelated films). Of the ones of direct lineage *$10,000 Blood Money* (1966), *Django Get A Coffin Ready* (1968) and *Django The Bastard* (1969) are all worthy successors, while *Django Kill* (1967) just nicks the name.

The Verdict: All Corbucci's most famous (and infamous) motifs are here - the extremely cruel violence, the larger-than-life characters, the hero's brief but emotive (and ultimately doomed) relationship with a girl, a hopelessly one-sided finale and a pessimistic, twist ending. Muddy brilliance. 5/5

The Hellbenders (1966)

Director Sergio Corbucci

Cast: Joseph Cotton (Colonel Jonas), Norma Bengell (Clare), Julian Mateos (Ben), Al Mulock (Beggar) 88 minutes

Story: In the years following the Civil War Jonas, an ex-Confederate Colonel, and his three sons steal a shipment of Yankee gold. With it they plan to resurrect the Confederacy. They pose as a funeral escort with Clare, a prostitute, impersonating the 'deceased's' wife; the money is hidden in the coffin. Their ruse works, as they avoid Yankee patrols and Sheriffs' posses and are saved by the army from a bandit gang, until finally their goal, the Hondo River, is in sight. But they are almost robbed by a beggar and one of the sons rapes and murders an Indian girl. The sons have been at each others throats throughout and this atrocity is the last straw. In a final shoot-out, all the brothers are left dead or dying, Clare has pneumonia and Jonas is mortally wounded. Even worse, Jonas makes the horrible discovery that it was all for nought. The coffin contains the corpse of an executed bandit. The money's been mistakenly buried by the Union army.

Background: An audacious change of pace from Corbucci, following the madness of *Django*. *The Hellbenders*, an anti-racist, anti-militarist diatribe, was a cross between a mission/heist movie (will they deliver the cash-leaden hearse to the rebels?) and a lamentation of the South's fate following the Civil War. Jonas and his three sons are used throughout to represent different aspects of the Confederacy (greed, compassion, jealousy, racism) while the coffin (and the mock deceased) jokingly stands for the South itself (hoping one day to 'rise again'). Even more disrespectful, Corbucci has the dead soldier's wife impersonated by a prostitute. Incidentally, the Hellbenders was the nickname of the regiment Jonas commanded during the Civil War.

The best performance of the film is obviously from the ever-talented Joseph Cotton. Ex of Orson Welles' Mercury Theatre Project, and involved in milestones *Citizen Kane* (1941), *The Magnificent Ambersons* (1942) and *The Third Man* (1949), Cotton must have wondered what the hell had happened when he found himself in Spain making Spaghetti Westerns. Jonas is the most complex character in the movie, completely besotted with 'The Cause' and blind to the disintegration of his clan. Cotton's haggard portrayal is completely convincing. Astoundingly, it was Cotton's second foray into Spaghettis. *The Hellbenders* was the sequel to *The Tramplers* (1966), which also starred Cotton as an ex-Confederate - the flamboyantly named Temple Cordine, head of the Cordine clan, who distributes justice by lynching anyone who doesn't agree with his racist, redundant views. In both films, Cotton's character is opposed by one of his sons, who tries (unsuccessfully) to make him change his ways.

The great things in *The Hellbenders*' favour? Corbucci's sick sense of the bizarre, Morricone's mournful 'Death Of The South' trumpet score and a really cruel twist ending. The premise of the coffin containing a dead soldier, but really brimming with stolen cash, was an idea borrowed from Leone's *The Good, The Bad And The Ugly*, but Corbucci uses it in a completely original way. The riverside robbery that descends into massacre at the beginning of *The Hellbenders* is the only recognisably Corbucci-esque moment, the rest of the movie consists of the family's efforts to trick their way past various groups - a posse, the army, some bandits, a priest and the Indians. These encounters are tension-filled, but tension is not what the director does best, nor what his audiences expect. In a very sick joke, Corbucci even has Jonas and his hearse encounter one of the dead hero's old comrades (now on pension), but 'luckily' he turns out to be blind and so can't identify Clare as an impostor. Cotton made one more Spaghetti called *White Comanche* (1968) which starred another unexpected Anglo refugee - William Shatner, who'd just appeared in the *Star Trek* TV series and must have thought he'd really reached the final frontier when he landed in Almeria.

The Verdict: The presence of Cotton makes this watchable, but the number of rip-offs released hot on the heels of *The Hellbenders* (exactly none) gives a fair idea of its impact on the Spaghetti Western craze. 3/5

The Hills Run Red (1966)

Director Carlo Lizzani

Cast: Thomas Hunter (Brewster), Henry Silva (Mendez), Dan Duryea (Getz), Nando Gazzalo (Seagal), Nicoletta Machiavelli (Mary-Ann) 89 minutes

Story: In the aftermath of the American Civil War, Jerry Brewster and Ken Seagal, two Confederate outlaws, are on the run with a fortune in Yankee cash. About to be captured, they agree to split up - Seagal takes the money (and promises to look after his partner's wife and child), while Brewster is captured and taken prisoner. After five years behind bars he returns home, but his ranch house is derelict, his wife dead and his son is missing. He vows revenge on Seagal and teams up with Winny Getz, a mysterious gunslinger. Brewster discovers that Seagal is now a rich landowner at war with a local saloon owner, Horner, over the lush grassland that surrounds Austin. Brewster sides with Horner in an effort to kill Seagal. As part of their plan, Brewster and Getz infiltrate Seagal's gang and cross the path of Garcia Mendez, Seagal's psychopathic henchman. Brewster also encounters his son, Tim, and Seagal's beautiful sister Mary-Ann. In a showdown, Mendez and his gang wipe out Horner's men and Brewster is unmasked as a traitor. Brewster and Getz ambush Mendez and Brewster kills Seagal in a duel. Getz reveals that he's a Government agent, on the trail of the stolen money, but even though he knows that Brewster was one of the robbers, he allows him to settle down with Mary-Ann and Tim, as Sheriff of Austin.

Background: Director Lizzani is better known for his more serious political Thrillers *Wake Up And Kill* (1966) and *The Violent Four* (1968) than his Spaghetti Westerns, though *The Hills Run Red* is one of the best examples of the genre. Written by Dean Craig, the film has a terrible, cliché-ridden script ('Lookee yonder', 'Doggawn' and 'Stay as still as a cactus' being the worst offenders), but is saved in just about every other department. The cast is amazing, a really unusual mix of newcomers and familiar Western faces. Unknown Thomas Hunter, as the hero, makes the most of his role and does an excellent imitation of Steve McQueen (in *Magnificent Seven* mode), whilst both Duryea and Silva appeared in many classic Hollywood Westerns - Duryea played Waco Johnny Dean in *Winchester 73*, oriental-looking Silva was vicious outlaw Chink in *The Tall T*. Silva is the most memorable aspect of the film. Dressed entirely in black leather, he dominates every scene as he intimidates (and just plain scares) other members of the cast at regular intervals with his screaming, unhinged histrionics. His persona was highly influential - in one scene he strides into a saloon, shouts 'Hasta La Vista' and opens fire on the patrons (years before Schwarzenegger appropriated the line and added 'Baby').

The Hills Run Red bears the unmistakable stamp of fifties psychological revenge Westerns (like *The Naked Spur*, *The Man From Laramie* and *Ride Lonesome*), but updates their ideals for the sixties. There is more sentiment in evidence than in Leone's films (particularly with the relationship between Brewster and his angelic son), but Lizzani knows where to draw the line and the last section of the film is an amazing series of action sequences - a canyon ambush, a saloon massacre and a massed gunfight in Austin - where stunts, gags and sheer imagination take over. In another more visceral moment Brewster voluntarily has the tattoo dedicated to his wife cut from his arm with a knife.

The film explores themes from *A Fistful Of Dollars* (the warring clans scenario), *For A Few Dollars More* (the younger Brewster joining forces with seasoned veteran Getz) and *Django* (the death of the hero's wife), but also anticipates Sergio Sollima's treatment of personality changes in *Face To Face*. The end of *The Hills Run Red* features a reformed outlaw being allowed to go free, even though the lawman knows he's a guilty man. Brewster's moral rehabilitation even extends to him being made sheriff. Morricone's score (including the effective ballad 'Home To My Love') has been little heard, but is up to his usual excellent standard, while the same can't be said for Lizzani's other Western *Requiescant* (1967, aka *Kill And Pray*), which is best avoided.

The Verdict: A highly imaginative action movie and a cracking take on fifties Westerns with a sixties twist, this is one largely overlooked movie that thoroughly deserves a cult following. 4/5

Navajo Joe (1966)

Director Sergio Corbucci

Cast: Burt Reynolds (Joe), Aldo Sambrell (Duncan), Nicoletta Machiavelli (Estella), Fernando Rey (Brother Jonathan) 89 minutes

Story: A gang of scalphunters, led by a sadistic half-breed named Duncan, are ravaging the countryside, indiscriminately attacking Indian camps and massacring their inhabitants (men and women alike) for the bounty of a dollar a scalp. When the bounties are suddenly withdrawn, they begin to attack local white townships, but a mysterious Indian named Joe intervenes and tries to help the whites. A local doctor is in league with the bandits and tips them off about a train loaded with cash. The bandits steal the cash, but the Indian foils the robbery and returns the money to the town of Esperanza. The bandits arrive and capture Joe after he has hidden the money. But the hero is freed when a young Indian girl decides to help him. Duncan and the bandits take the whole town prisoner, keeping them locked up in the church, but the Indian lures the scalphunters away into the desert. Having gradually decimated the gang, Joe faces the remaining members until only Duncan is left alive. During the climactic duel in an Indian burial ground, Duncan learns that he killed and scalped Joe's wife in one of his raids. Joe kills Duncan but is mortally wounded and sends the money back to Esperanza on his horse, while he remains in the graveyard and prepares to meet his ancestors.

Background: This is one of future superstar Burt Reynolds' first successful starring roles, though he often cites it as his worst movie. He's wrong, as anyone who's sat through *At Long Last Love* (1975), *Smokey And The Bandit 2* (1980) and *Stroker Ace* (1983) will no doubt attest. Corbucci's sixth Western is one of his best, not least for Reynolds' rippling portrayal of feathers and leathers Joe, who whittles down the huge gang of scalphunters single-handed. Reynolds hardly says a word for the first half of the movie (and when he does it's in a very basic, "Me Tarzan, you Jane", style), but as far as performances go, this is one of Reynolds' better efforts. Like Eastwood, he was appearing in American TV Westerns (like *Gunsmoke* and *Riverboat*) when he was cast in 1966 in a film with the working title *A Dollar A Head*. Though it failed to catapult Reynolds to superstardom and he left Italy before shooting was finished, Corbucci managed a pretty good cut-and-paste job. One of the most distinctive and successful aspects of *Navajo Joe* is the incredible screaming, clanging score by Ennio Morricone. The music incorporates much Indian-style yelling and whooping, as well as several effectively understated flute-led compositions that enhance Reynolds' on-screen relationship with the beautiful Indian maiden, Estella - played by the stunning Italian actress Nicoletta Machiavelli, in her most memorable role.

Navajo Joe is a more overtly 'message' film than Corbucci had previously attempted. He abandoned the underlying racism of *Django* and *The Hellbenders* (both of which concentrated on Post-Civil War Southerners attempting to continue the conflict) and made his villain a full-blown, Indian-hating bastard. In the chilling opening sequence, half-breed scalphunter Duncan stops near an Indian encampment and smiles at a young girl washing her clothes, before, without warning, shooting her dead and scalping her. His psychological unbalances are explained in an effective scene later, when he describes why he hates whites (like his father) and Indians (like his mother) - the first time a Corbucci villain got the opportunity to explain himself.

The film is exceptionally violent for its time and is still one of Corbucci's most graphic movies - included are some vicious beatings, convincing stunts (supervised by ex-stuntman Reynolds) and death by tomahawk, bullet, knife, scalpel and strangulation. The relationship between Joe and his obedient horse is a brief concession by Corbucci to traditional Hollywood Westerns (his mount even carries the money back to town in lieu of Joe), though other aspects of the movie (the Indian hero, the downbeat ending) are obviously influenced by bleaker, more considered fifties Indian Westerns, including Burt Lancaster's action-packed *Apache* (1954), the brutal *The Last Wagon* (1956) and Kirk Douglas' *The Indian Fighter* (1955).

The Verdict: Reynolds said this film was so bad that it was only shown in prisons and aeroplanes because no one could leave - "I killed 10,000 guys, wore a Japanese slingshot and a fright wig." Ignore Reynolds' opinion. 4/5

A Stranger In Town (1966)

Director Luigi Vanzi

Cast: Tony Anthony (The Stranger), Frank Wolff (Aguila) 84 minutes

Story: A fast-drawing stranger arrives in a desolate Mexican border settlement and witnesses a bandit gang, led by their sadistic leader Aguila, wipe out a company of Mexican Federales and make off with their uniforms. The stranger joins the band to steal a gold shipment from the US Army, but he's double-crossed and beaten. Facing the gang alone, he picks them off one by one and kills Aguila, before returning the money to the US Army.

Background: If the story seems familiar, that's because it is. This is by far the most blatant rip-off of *A Fistful Of Dollars*, compounded even further by its alternate title, *For A Dollar In The Teeth*. Not only does Vanzi use a simplified version of the same plot, but Anthony plays a nameless stranger dressed exactly like Eastwood's poncho-wearing stranger and sucks meanly on cigars. But this film had American backing (it's a US/Spanish co-production) and like Eastwood's *Hang 'Em High* (1968), it represents an American's idea of a Spaghetti Western - short on plot and characterisation, long on violence. But the whole package (including an absolutely appalling performance by Wolff in the Ramon Rojo role) is so poorly executed that its success, especially in America, is difficult to fathom. The finale is memorable however. In *A Fistful Of Dollars* the stranger uses a square of iron cut from an old mining railcar as a makeshift bulletproof vest. In *A Stranger In Town* the hero uses a whole railcar, (which runs on tracks down the main street) as he faces Aguila, who is armed with a machine-gun.

The film's success made Anthony a star and resulted in two Stranger sequels - *The Stranger Returns* (1967) and *The Silent Stranger* (1969) both directed by Vanzi, and several other similar outings, including the surreal *Blindman* (1971), Anthony's best film. If *The Silent Stranger* (wherein the stranger found himself in Japan) was the weakest of the Stranger trilogy, then *The Stranger Returns* was the most accomplished. Also called *A Man A Horse A Gun* and *Shoot First Laugh Last* this is more imaginative and better plotted than its predecessor, set in a truly Wild West. Anthony's stranger (again in a poncho) tracks down a renegade (played by Italian strongman Dan Vadis) and his gang, known as the Treasure of the Border because of the massive bounty on their heads. The bandits steal a solid gold stagecoach (yes, you read it right) and the stranger gets beaten up and dragged behind the coach before levelling the gang with his four-barrelled shotgun. But the details of the film (which is more parodic and less slavishly imitative than *A Stranger In Town*) work a lot better. The stranger sunbathes under a pink parasol, has a natty sidekick (called the Prophet) with a box full of fireworks, christens his horse Pussy (which makes for some rather strange dialogue) and never finishes his ineptly rolled cigarettes - they taste so bad.

The Verdict: The most successful imitators of the Eastwood movies, the Stranger films show just how much of a powerful and popular icon a poncho-draped hero had become in the sixties. *A Stranger In Town* 2/5, *The Stranger Returns* 3/5

51

Box-Office Dynamite: 1967-69

Death Rides A Horse (1967)

Director Giulio Petroni

Cast: Lee Van Cleef (Ryan), John Phillip Law (Bill), Luigi Pistilli (Walcott), Anthony Dawson (Cavanaugh) 110 minutes

Story: At a lonely way-station on a stormy night, an outlaw gang rob a cash shipment resting there overnight. During the raid, four members of the gang attack the ranch house, killing the owner, his wife and teenage daughter - but a fifth man saves the rancher's little son. Fifteen years later this little boy, named Bill, has grown up and plots revenge on the outlaws. He is joined in his vendetta by a mysterious gunslinger Ryan, recently released from prison, who also has a score to settle with the gang. The pair track down and kill the first bandit, Cavanaugh, who is now a respectable saloon owner. The next is Walcott, who is now a banker. He has been entrusted with a million dollars worth of public funds and the rest of the murderers are his gang. Walcott steals the money and gets the authorities to blame Ryan (who used to be a member of Walcott's gang, but was betrayed). Walcott hides out in a Mexican village and eventually Ryan and Bill, with the help of the local peasants, defeat him. In the dénouement, it transpires that Ryan was present the night Bill's family were killed and it was he who saved Bill's life. Though Bill holds Ryan partly responsible for not stopping the massacre, he decides not to kill his partner.

Background: This was the first and most successful of a series of big-budget remakes of *For A Few Dollars More*. *Death Rides A Horse* can at least be excused accusations of plagiarism, as it was written by Luciano Vincenzoni (who scripted Leone's film) and again starred cadaverous Van Cleef, as the older half of a pair of gunslingers who team up to catch the bandits. The connection was further stressed by the casting of Luigi Pistilli as chief villain, Walcott. Pistilli had played a prominent member of Indio's gang in *For A Few Dollars More*. For the younger hero, previously portrayed by Clint Eastwood, director Petroni cast American John Phillip Law, who remains best known for his roles as an intergalactic angel in *Barbarella: Queen Of The Galaxy* (1967) and the super-thief hero in *Danger: Diabolik* (1968). But unfortunately this casting decision is the weak link in the film, as Law is no Eastwood.

That said, the film is still impressively staged. Anyone familiar with *For A Few Dollars More* will enjoy recognising Petroni's blatant inspiration. Every aspect of Leone's film is present and correct - even down to the red-tinted flashbacks to the night of horror, the uneasy partnership between young and old, a prison break (using a locomotive instead of dynamite) and the final, apocalyptic shoot-out in a Mexican village (very reminiscent of *The Magnificent Seven*). *Death Rides A Horse* also marked a shift in the role of the villains and was the first Spaghetti to pit Van Cleef against a bunch of outlaws who have adopted masks of respectability. Here the villains have used their ill-gotten gains to set themselves up as 'righteous men' and Van Cleef must oust them from power before dealing with them in his own inimitable way (i.e. shooting them to pieces). This theme permeated all Van Cleef's subsequent sixties Westerns.

Death Rides A Horse is exceptionally violent (especially the opening sequence) and Ennio Morricone's harsh, chanted score emphasises this. At one point young Law is buried up to his neck in sand, has salt pushed in his mouth and is left to die in the desert, while in another scene he is tortured by having his head trapped in a huge grain press. Not to be outdone, Van Cleef gets badly beaten up by the bandits before getting his revenge. Stranger however was the fact that despite such savagery, the film was released uncut outside Europe in 1969. In an interesting footnote, the other main villain was played by British actor Anthony Dawson, who had played the killer hired by Ray Milland to bump off his wife (Grace Kelly) in Hitchcock's *Dial M For Murder* (1953) and also had small roles in three James Bond movies - *Dr No*, *From Russia With Love* and *Thunderball*. In *Death Rides A Horse* he played 'Four Aces' Cavanaugh, so called because of the distinctive four Ace playing cards tattooed on his chest.

The Verdict: Though this looks exactly like a Leone film and is heavily indebted to *For A Few Dollars More* it holds its own with the best Spaghettis. The epitome of the Italian revenge Western and one of Van Cleef's finest. 4/5

Face To Face (1967)

Director Sergio Sollima

Cast: Gian Maria Volonte (Brad), Tomas Milian (Beau), William Berger (Siringo), Jolanda Modio (Maria), Gianni Rizzo (Williams) 107 minutes

Story: Tubercular Professor of History Brad Fletcher resigns from his post at an Eastern university and goes West to convalesce. He inadvertently aids the escape of a notorious half-breed bandit, Beauregard Bennett, and finds himself drawn to the outlaw's brutal, amoral life. So much so that when Beau reforms his old gang to terrorise the Southwest once more, Brad joins them. Among Beau's recruits is a newcomer named Charley

Siringo, who isn't a bandit but a lawman working for the Pinkerton's Detective Agency. His mission is to track down Beau and break up the gang. Whilst they hide out with some renegades in the hills (where the locals fete Beau as a folk hero), Brad gradually loses his Eastern conscience and eventually is accepted into the gang. He undermines Beau's leadership, but his first robbery, a bank hold-up, is a chaotic failure - Siringo sells them out, the gang are wiped out and Beau is captured. Only Brad escapes unscathed. Brad sets himself up in the outlaws hideout as a king and recruits a bigger, more brutal gang of ruffians. But the authorities send an army of vigilantes to wipe out the hideout for good. Beau escapes and rejoins Brad, but not before the entire outlaw community has been ravaged by the posse. Siringo intervenes and halts the vigilantes before they can kill Beau and Brad. Brad wounds Siringo, but Beau then kills Brad, before being allowed to go free by the lawman, who sees that Beau has changed and Beau Bennett the ruthless outlaw no longer exists.

Background: Following the success of *The Big Gundown*, Sollima went on to make this film, which he regards as his own personal favourite. The basic plot is incredibly similar to *The Big Gundown*'s (a bandit on the run with a lawman on his trail), but *Face To Face* is a much more complex film. Often touted as a parable of the rise of Italian Fascism, Sollima denied this and said that the film was about the changes that can occur when different personalities are transposed to different environments (becoming civilised amongst civilised men, violent among the violent). Instead of concentrating on the relationship between the outlaw (Beau) and the lawman (Siringo), Sollima replaced the groups encountered by Cuchillo in *The Big Gundown* (the Mormons, the Widow's henchmen, the Monks) and had the outlaw on the run encounter an educated, cowardly professor (Brad). This culture shock forms the centre of the movie. Brad gradually learns how to be an outlaw, whilst Beau learns that there is more to life than robbing banks and killing lawmen.

The film also draws on many historical sources (the James gang, the plight of the South following the Civil War) and seamlessly interweaves some important political and social observations (including the exploitation of the masses, the moral acceptability of war and the professor's quest to 'go down in history') - again without setting the action in the Mexican Revolution. The film has shortcomings: it is far too talky and some of the peripheral characters are sketchily drawn (in sharp contrast with their equivalents in *The Big Gundown*). Ennio Morricone's score is by turns fittingly moving and aptly vicious and the three leads are perfectly cast. Milian, with an Apache Indian-style haircut and buckskins, gives what many believe is his best Western performance, while Berger does an excellent job of the lawman, a part destined to be played by Lee Van Cleef. But the real revelation is Volonte, a stage actor, who had previously played Mexican bandits in the first two Dollars films and Damiani's *A Bullet For The General*. Here, as the suave but naïve Easterner-out-West, he injects pathos and depth into a performance that could easily have been highly unconvincing. Sollima's vision is unique and the epic sweep of the film transcends Spaghetti Westerns of the time - especially in the last quarter of the film, when the vigilantes are let loose on the outlaws' hideout. And as well as the philosophising about education, death, morality and trust, there are plenty of gunfights to please the shoot-em-up fans. The failed heist is an excellently choreographed street fight (akin to the James gangs' Northfield bank raid) and the finale is a familiar Leone-esque three-way shootout. As is usual with Sollima's Westerns, beware the abridged version, which lost 15 minutes of footage, a couple of showdowns and quite a large chunk of Beau and Brad's relationship.

The Verdict: The confrontation between the pistol and the mind makes this a Spaghetti Western with brains, even if they are sometimes splattered over the screen. 4/5

The Big Silence (1967)

Director Sergio Corbucci

Cast: Jean Louis Trintignant (Silence), Klaus Kinski (Loco), Vonetta McGee (Pauline), Luigi Pistilli (Pollicut) 100 minutes

Story: In the snowy wastes of Utah, outlaws hide in the mountains to avoid being captured by a vicious gang of bounty hunters led by Loco. When a local woman, Pauline, loses her husband to Loco's band, she sends for Silence, a mute gunfighter who defends outlaws against Loco's tyranny. But when Silence arrives in the town of Snow Hill, he also has a score to settle with the crooked Justice of the Peace, Pollicut, the man responsible for him being mute - when Silence was a child, his parents were killed and because he was a witness he had his throat slit, rendering him speechless. Silence shoots off one of Pollicut's thumbs, so he can't fire a pistol. In retribution, Pollicut hires Loco to kill Silence, but in a shoot-out, Loco's gang are decimated. Silence is wounded, then nursed back to health by Pauline. Later, Pollicut cripples Silence's hands, at the cost of his own life, while Loco captures the outlaws from the hills. In the final showdown, Silence attempts to save the outlaws, but he and Pauline are callously shot down by Loco and his men, who then turn on the outlaws and massacre them to a man.

Background: Drawing on influences like André de Toth's stark *Day Of The Outlaw* (1959) and Mario Bava's snowy 'Wurdalak' episode of *Black Sabbath* (1963), *The Big Silence* is one of the most beautiful and imaginative Spaghetti Westerns, though it is also the most downbeat. Even Corbucci's own bleak movies hadn't gone as far as letting the baddies win, but that is what happens here. Instead of the muddy town of *Django*, Snow Hill is a desolate, snowbound place, suspended in clouds of fog, where vicious bounty hunters run the show - a poke by Corbucci at Leone's heroic bounty killers. The film echoes *A Fistful Of Dollars* (in the inter-gang conflict between the outlaws and the bounty hunters) and *Django* (with the revenge sub-plot and the love story between Silence and Pauline) but the thought that went into its execution transcends the genre. With Morricone's delicate, plaintive score (the antithesis of his Dollars music) echoing the falling snow, the film unfolds in classic style.

French actor Trintignant, a continental sex symbol since the success of the love story *A Man And A Woman* the previous year, is perfect as the mute avenger, Silence, wrapped up against the cruel winter and armed with a rapid-firing Mauser machine-pistol, with detachable shoulder stock - a flashy variation of Django's machine-gun. Pistilli is equally effective as the jumpy, thumbless Justice of the Peace, a nasty racist who was responsible for Silence's silence. Negress Vonetta McGee's touching portrayal adds depth to the hopeless love affair that develops during Silence's convalescence. But it is Kinski, as the villainous bounty hunter Loco, who walks away with the movie. His shrouded face looks like a Horror movie grotesque, as he stalks the snowy hills, seeking out his prey. It is his best Western performance and one of the finest of his career, his more critically acclaimed work for Werner Herzog included. He guns down starving outlaws with barely concealed relish and then packs their bodies in ice to be transported on the roof of the stagecoach. By chance, Loco (called Tigrero or 'The Tiger' in the Italian version) and Silence begin the film sharing a stagecoach ride to Snow Hill and though the conversation is a little one-sided, it sets the central antagonism up perfectly, as the coach winds its way through the beautiful snowscape.

The violent action sequences are amongst the best Corbucci staged. But the horror of the flashback (where Silence as a boy has his throat slit) and the moment when Pollicut has his thumb shot off contrast well with the unusual explicitness of Silence and Pauline's love for one another, the most impressive depiction of love in a Corbucci Western. The director's powerful imagery - including blood dripping on the snow from corpses' wounds, the rag-clothed scythe-carrying outlaws (who haunt the hills and feast on dead horses), a man drowned on a frozen lake (plunging through the ice to his death) and Silence's long silent scream when his hands are scorched on open coals - propels this film from the relative cheapness of Corbucci's previous efforts, *Django* and *Navajo Joe*, and into Leone's league. And the nihilistic finale lives long in the memory - a moment when a man has to do what a man has to do, over love, the odds and all reasonable logic.

Though not especially influential on Spaghettis (a few picked up on the snowbound locale), it is the most influential Spaghetti (outside the Dollars films) on Clint Eastwood's career back in American Westerns. Ideas, props and whole scenes appear unchanged in *Hang 'Em High* (1967), *Joe Kidd* (1972) and *Unforgiven* (1992), films that were often over-praised for their originality, such is Corbucci's hidden legacy.

The Verdict: Silence was golden at the European box office, but like *Django* it wasn't released in Britain or the US - the ending was too pessimistic for their audiences' sensibilities. But that is *The Big Silence*'s power - a kick in the teeth, when other directors gave their fans a reassuring lift. But which technique is most effective? Snow contest. 5/5

Django Kill - If You Live Shoot! (1967)

Director Giulio Questi

Cast: Tomas Milian (The Stranger), Piero Lulli (Oaks), Roberto Camardiel (Zorro), Paco Sanz (Hagerman), Milo Quesada (Tembler) 115 minutes

Story: Two Indian mystics find a half-dying stranger in the desert and nurse him back to health. He has been left for dead by his comrades, a bandit gang led by Oaks, who have stolen a Union gold shipment. Oaks and his men arrive in a violent town and are attacked and killed by the locals, led by Tembler the saloon-keeper and Hagerman the storekeeper. The pair then split the gold between them. The stranger and the Indians arrive and decide to stick around and track down the haul, while a Mexican rancher named Zorro and his gang are also after the cache. The violence escalates until Hagerman kills Tembler and blames it on the stranger, after the storekeeper has buried the gold in the cemetery. Zorro captures and crucifies the stranger (in a cage full of vampire bats), but the stranger frees himself and defeats Zorro and his gang. Hagerman now has all the gold and hides it in a beam in his house, but the building catches fire and he dies, gilded in molten gold, leaving the stranger to ride out with nothing.

Background: Over the years *Django Kill* has gained a reputation as the most violent Spaghetti Western and though the film has tempered with age, it's still one of the oddest genre contributions. Several film-makers in the sixties and seventies experimented with the form of the Western, with varying degrees of success. Maverick artist Andy Warhol made *Lonesome Cowboys* (1968) predictably with the emphasis on transvestites, bisexuality and camp parody, Dennis Hopper made *The Last Movie* (1971) a loose, improvisational film deconstructing the mythology of Westerns, and Alexandro Jodorowsky made the strangest 'Western' of all time, *El Topo* (1971) - a rambling, Biblical odyssey that lampooned John Wayne, religion, mysticism and Sergio Leone, whilst killing a lot of animals in the name of 'Head-movie' entertainment.

Questi's *Django Kill* is the most recognisably Western of the bunch, though the extreme violence, mystical Indian waffle and bizarre characters still set the film apart from Leone, Tessari et al, and even from the excesses of Sergio Corbucci.

The film is loosely based on *A Fistful Of Dollars* (two gangs, a cache of gold, a lone stranger), but it also wanders into Edgar Allan Poe Horror, Jane Eyre-inspired melodrama and dark twisted sexuality. Like Corbucci's *Django*, the two gangs in town are not your typical Western fare. The townsmen are led by Hagerman, a pious zealot (who keeps his wife locked in her bedroom with bars on the windows) and Tembler (who has a gang of self-righteous, stranger-hating toughs, who hang around his bar). The Mexicans are led by jovial, bewhiskered Zorro, quite literally a Gay Calabrero who has a psychic parrot and a gang of honchos (his 'Muchachos') dressed in identical black suits - an idea lifted wholesale from an earlier Spaghetti called *Three Golden Boys* (1966). Moreover, Zorro fancies his own men. These protagonists sound interesting enough (almost the ingredients for a send-up), but Questi's unrelentingly violent vision and complete lack of humour make this a film that takes itself far too seriously. Its unusual content was taken very seriously by the censors and it lost over 20 minutes of footage when the movie finally made it outside mainland Europe in 1970, though many of the deletions trimmed extended dialogue scenes about the afterlife between the stranger and his Indian companions.

But the violence, especially in the uncut version (or as close to uncut as the censors will allow), is still disturbing. Horses are hacked with machetes and later blown to bits with dynamite (the aftermath being particularly harrowing) and the saloon-keeper's son is sexually assaulted by Zorro's Muchachos. The stranger's love interest is burnt to a crisp in the *Fall Of The House Of Usher*-inspired finale, which also sees Hagerman swathed in molten gold. Among the other grotesqueries are a savage mass lynching and two scenes that are cut from all available versions of the film - an Indian is scalped by the townspeople (an ironic reversal of usual Western 'etiquette') and Oaks' chest is torn apart during an operation, when it's discovered he's been riddled with golden bullets. Moreover, the stranger - after being shot and left for dead - has to endure a crucifixion (in a prison cell which vampire bats and lizards call home). Questi includes much religious imagery and mystical mumbo-jumbo about the Land of the Dead, and the whole film works as a rumination of Heaven and Hell, death and rebirth. But his style is so erratic that this film belongs in a different universe to the other Spaghetti Westerns, far closer to *El Topo* and Warhol's juxtaposed underground cinema.

The Verdict: Sure, it's startlingly original and magnificently photographed, but for some reason *Django Kill* doesn't gel in the same way as *Django* or other less mainstream offerings. Tomas Milian (in his first starring role) is excellent as the half-breed stranger and many of the sequences are genuinely surreal (including the entrance of Oaks' gang into town - a deeply unsettling highlight), but this is an out-of-control, sick Pop-Art fantasy of a West that only ever existed in Questi's delirious (but very imaginative) mind. 3/5

Day Of Anger (1967)

Director Tonino Valerii

Cast: Lee Van Cleef (Talby), Giuliano Gemma (Scott), Walter Rilla (Murph), Al Mulock (Wild Jack) 110 minutes

Story: In the town of Clifton, a young orphan named Scott Mary is victimised by the townspeople. When ageing outlaw Frank Talby rides into town, Scott sees the opportunity to break free from their oppression and teams up with the gunman, who educates him as a shootist. Talby, recently released from jail, meets with his old partner Wild Jack, who owes him the takings from their last robbery in Abilene. Jack says he hasn't got the loot as he was double-crossed by his associates, who were all respectable men from Clifton - the Judge, the saloon-keeper, the banker and an army officer. Now they have the cash. Talby kills Jack and returns with Scott to Clifton to exact his revenge. They blackmail the various dignitaries and set themselves up as rich, influential men. But as Talby goes power-crazy, Scott comes into conflict with his only friend in town, Murph an ex-Sheriff with a score to settle with Talby. Eventually seeing sense, Scott faces Talby, after Talby has killed Murph in cold blood. In a showdown Scott defeats Talby and his cronies using the lessons that Talby once taught him.

Background: A formula Van Cleef vehicle with all the necessary ingredients - Van Cleef rides into town, gets double-crossed, gets nasty and gets his revenge, with the added twist that he gets killed for his trouble. While Clint Eastwood returned to the States to pursue a career in his native land, Van Cleef became the number one star of Spaghetti Westerns on the continent. For his fifth he was yet again involved in a film that drew heavily on the plot and characters of *For A Few Dollars More* (his Italian debut in 1965). Van Cleef reprised his role of an ageing gunman hooked up with a younger sidekick (this time Gemma), except that now their relationship was that of master gunman and protégé. Like *Death Rides A Horse* (1967) Van Cleef and his partner find themselves against a bunch of outlaws now deemed honest citizens as a result of their crimes, but in a slight plot twist, Van Cleef sets about blackmailing them into submission. Unfortunately, as each man outlives his usefulness, Van Cleef kills them, until he is the town tyrant, forcing a confrontation with his young partner.

Gemma's characterisation as Scott the young orphan (reduced in the film's opening to collecting barrels of shit from the local businesses, in a primitive form of effluent recycling) adds a new dimension to the action. He is ostensibly a good guy who under Talby's guidance becomes a lethal hired gun. Throughout the film, Talby teaches Scott a series of lessons (the 'rules of the game'), before turning him against the town he hates. By the end, Scott's conscience tells him to side with his elderly guardian Murph - an honourable man. This conflict between good and evil is the centre of the film.

Day Of Anger was directed by Valerii, who began as assistant to Leone on the first two Dollars films. He then directed an excellent bounty hunter Western *For The Taste Of Killing* (1966), which reused sets and ideas from Leone's *For A Few Dollars More* - a trend that continued with *Day Of Anger*. If possible see the uncut 110-minute version of the film as the video releases (as *Days Of Wrath* and *Gunlaw*) are missing 20 minutes of footage, including much violence and character development. This abridged version looks like an excuse for Van Cleef to mow down the population of a town, while the full version tells you why. The score by Riz Ortolani is a jangly, jazzy workout that bears little resemblance to Morricone's scores, while the performances (especially Gemma and Al Mulock from *The Good, The Bad And The Ugly*) are pretty convincing.

The Verdict: Van Cleef seems to be going through the Spaghetti Western motions but it's still worth a look. Avoid the cut version, or you'll wonder why this gets 3/5

Once Upon A Time In The West (1968)

Director Sergio Leone

Cast: Claudia Cardinale (Jill), Henry Fonda (Frank), Charles Bronson (Harmonica), Jason Robards (Cheyenne), Gabriele Ferzetti (Morton) 159 minutes

Story: In the desolate Southwest, Frank, a gunman in the pay of crippled railroad tycoon Morton, massacres the McBain family in a bid to secure the land they own - so that the railway they are constructing can continue towards the Pacific. But soon afterwards McBain's recently-wed wife Jill arrives from New Orleans and tries to figure out who killed her husband. The crime is blamed on an outlaw named Cheyenne, who pleads his innocence. Meanwhile a mysterious Harmonica-playing gunman appears on the scene and protects Jill from further attempts on her life by Frank's ruffians. Through recurring flashbacks it transpires that Harmonica has a vendetta to settle with Frank. Eventually Jill is captured by Frank and is forced to auction her land, but Harmonica intervenes and buys the land, using Cheyenne's bounty as payment. Morton, realising that Frank is starting to usurp his position buys off Frank's men and turns them against their boss. Frank survives and, discovering Morton dying as a result of an attack by Cheyenne's men, goes gunning for Harmonica. As the rail gangs arrive at Jill's ranch, Frank faces Harmonica and discovers that years before he killed Harmonica's brother. The avenger kills Frank and rides away with Cheyenne's body (who had been mortally wounded in the encounter with Morton's men), leaving Jill to look after the railroad workers at the ranch that will soon become a station.

Background: The Good, The Bad And The Ugly is Leone's most popular action-packed Spaghetti Western, but *Once Upon A Time In The West* is the critics' choice. With this film, Leone broke away from the Dollars films and attempted to make an authentically epic Western. Instead of reinventing the West as action cinema, Leone appropriated and adapted key moments from the genre and recycled them into the last word on the death of the West. It was a device that his contemporaries Duccio Tessari (with his Ringo films) and Sergio Sollima (with his political Westerns) had already done, but such nuances in their work had been largely overlooked. These directors deployed various Hollywood clichés (the drunken Sheriff, the crooked railroad tycoon, the Eastern dude, the square-jawed good guy, his swooning girl) and blended them into something new (to great box-office success). Leone and Sergio Donati took a similar approach. The original story was written by Leone and two young men soon to be directors in their own right - Bernardo Bertolucci (*The Conformist* and *Last Tango In Paris*) and Dario Argento (*The Bird With The*

Crystal Plumage and *Suspiria*). But their convoluted screenplay was pruned by Sergio Donati, who had already had much success with Sollima's thought-provoking Spaghettis *The Big Gundown* and *Face To Face*. Leone's film became a tribute to the Western itself, with the plot, the incidents and the characters taken wholesale from the landmarks of the genre. The plot of the railroad trying to get land to build on was as old as the hills, the revenge motif of 'you killed my brother' was equally hackneyed and the characters were similarly familiar.

But though *Once Upon A Time* is more critically lauded than the Dollars Trilogy, it is far less successful as a Spaghetti Western (a genre by now associated with fast action and much bloodletting) and bombed in America on its original release, while other Spaghettis continued to do fantastic business there. To some extent it was stylistically ahead of its time. It was also unusual for a Spaghetti Western to have a big-name international cast. Fonda, an actor Leone was after since *A Fistful Of Dollars*, was cast as Frank, a woman- and child-killing hired gun - an excessive variation on Lee Van Cleef's 'Angel Eyes' from *The Good, The Bad And The Ugly*, except that this time there is a reason for the gunman's activities. Now the shootist helps a slowly-dying capitalist clear the way for his dream of a railroad to the Pacific.

Bronson replaced Eastwood as the mysterious stranger and in so doing gave the best performance of his career. For once his stone-faced acting enhancing his portrayal; he's silent for much of the film, happier playing on his harmonica than talking to the other characters. Robards was adequate as a Tuco-esque outlaw, enhancing the 'trio' aspect of the story that echoed the dynamic of *The Good, The Bad And The Ugly*. But it was Jill and Mr Morton that really took the film beyond more established fare. For the first time Leone cast an actress in a leading role and created one of the most memorable heroines in Western history. Moreover, Cardinale's Jill epitomised the nascent optimism of Leone's post-Dollars West. It was a new West, a land that was now a nation evolving. From the wild expanse of the Dollars films, civilisation had finally caught up with the Spaghetti heroes and *Once Upon A Time In The West* showed them dealing with it. Harmonica can't understand this new West and rides away (like Eastwood would have), with the body of another character caught out of time (Cheyenne) slung over a horse. Frank tries to become a businessman, but realises he can never adapt to Morton's methods. He understands the power of guns but not the greater power of dollar bills. This is epitomised by the moment when Frank, outwitted by Harmonica at the auction, finds himself facing his own men. The tubercular Mr Morton adds another dimension to

Leone's fairy tale, though even he had his roots elsewhere - scriptwriter Donati had used similar characters in *The Good, The Bad And The Ugly* (a crippled prison camp commander) and *Face To Face* (a wheelchair-bound businessman). And even though he is a totally despicable character, Morton's death is one of the most moving moments in the Spaghetti Western genre - crawling towards a puddle of water in the middle of the desert, a pitiful substitute for the vastness of the Pacific.

Once Upon A Time In The West was an attempt by Leone at a Western to equal Ford, Hawks, Walsh, Sturges and the other old masters. The fact that only Westerns by Peckinpah, George Roy Hill and Eastwood (Leone's protégé) have made much impact on the genre since is testament to Leone's masterpiece. Most significant however is the power of the set pieces and their perfect fusion with Morricone's score (which many rate as his finest) - a masterclass in musical and cinematic technique. The opening scene is a long, largely silent title sequence as three of Frank's gunslingers (Jack Elam, Woody Strode and Al Mulock) wait *High Noon*-like for the train with Bronson on board. The next scene is the massacre at the McBain ranch, where Fonda and his men stride towards the house and gun down the entire family, with Morricone's harmonica and electric guitar theme jarring ominously on the soundtrack. The gangs' long duster coats immediately became hugely influential and duster-clad gunmen have epitomised this film ever since. The scenes of Jill riding on a buggy through the desert, cut to Morricone's soaring soprano piece remain unique among Leone's work. But it is the finale that really stays in the memory. The final duel between Frank and Harmonica begins and in the arena of death nothing that has happened in the film matters. Harmonica's flashback to his brother's death is breathtaking (and its stunning presentation almost overshadows the gunfight). Under a huge stone arch, in the middle of a plain, Harmonica's brother stands on Harmonica's shoulders, with a rope around his neck, as Frank sneers. The rope around Tuco's neck in *The Good, The Bad And The Ugly* (which was usually the excuse of a joke) has been replaced with the ultimate nightmare, a hideous Catch 22 - only Harmonica's strength can keep his brother alive. It is one of the most powerful images in the history of cinema.

The Verdict: Truth be told, this film has no place in a book on Spaghetti Westerns. Though it was made in Italy, the US (Monument Valley) and Spain, and reuses many of the actors, locations and themes of Spaghettis, it is about as far removed from the genre in 1968 as a Hollywood Western. Leone himself reiterated this. He didn't see this movie as a Spaghetti Western - the Spaghettis were the lower-budget, ultra-violent copyists (which to Leone was anyone except him). *Once Upon A Time In The West* was an Italian Western, a cynical, violent and yet reverential cultural comment on a genre and a nation. In fact over the years it has achieved the ultimate accolade and is now referred to simply as a 'Classic Western', with no mention of pasta. 5/5

A Professional Gun (1968)

Director Sergio Corbucci

Cast: Franco Nero (Kowalski), Tony Musante (Paco), Jack Palance (Curly), Giovanna Ralli (Columba), Eduardo Fajardo (Garcia) 100 minutes

Story: During the Mexican Revolution, Polak mercenary Kowalski is hired by a mine owner Garcia to escort silver from his mine in Sierra Palo, Mexico, to safety in Texas. But peasant mineworker Paco and his cohorts take control of the mine and join up with Kowalski to get rich from the revolution. Kowalski teaches Paco some elementary tactics as their band cut a swathe through Mexico and Paco soon becomes a popular leader of the revolution. But Garcia wants revenge and employs Curly, a gringo hired gun, to trap and kill Kowalski and Paco. Garcia, with an army detachment and artillery, attacks Paco's headquarters in Santa Rosita. Although it's a massacre, Kowalski, Paco and Columba (Paco's girl) escape. Curly catches up with them and is killed in a duel in a bullring. Garcia captures the Polak and Paco but before their execution they escape into the desert. The Polak wants to renew their partnership and join another revolution, but Paco is determined to continue fighting alongside his comrades in Mexico, so they go their separate ways.

Background: This is the first of Corbucci's Political Spaghetti trilogy that continued with *Compañeros* (1970) and *What Am I Doing In The Middle Of A Revolution?* (1972). All three are entertaining Mexico-set adventures incorporating the paraphernalia of modern warfare - machine-guns, grenades, motor cars, lorries, motorbikes (with sidecars) and biplanes - to excellent effect. Corbucci juxtaposed this gadgetry with the lowly peasant characters and their rural roots - a simple country existence to contrast with all the sophisticated hardware on display. In each of the movies there is a European character (a Polish mercenary, a Swedish gun-runner or an Italian stage actor) who becomes involved in the revolution, either intentionally (as in *Compañeros*) or purely by accident (the other two). *A Professional Gun* is the best of the trio and was hugely influential on the Mexican Revolutionary cycle of Westerns (both Italian and American) in the late sixties and early seventies - big movies about big stars blowing big chunks out of the Mexican countryside.

But *A Professional Gun* is much more intelligently put together than the wave of imitators that appeared in its wake. It was co-written by Luciano Vincenzoni (*For A Few Dollars More*, *The Good The Bad And The Ugly*, *Death Rides A Horse*) and again features a trio of characters - two good (Kowalski and Paco), one bad (hired gun Curly). It was based on a story partly written by Franco Solinas, who contributed to *A Bullet For The General* and *The Big Gundown*. It has an apt score by Morricone that incorporates Mexican-flavoured fiestas and darker, whistled themes. But the best aspects of the movie are the great-looking settings and the brilliant cast. Franco Nero (previously Corbucci's anti-hero par excellence in *Django*) was cast as the duster-wearing, bewhiskered Polak, Kowalski whose motto (when asked where his allegiances lie) is "I'm on my side." In an early sequence he visits an arms dealer and buys himself a Hawkins machine-gun (it would be ridiculous for Nero to appear in a Corbucci movie without one) and is the epitome of cool throughout. Apart from his calm professionalism (unmoved by any threatening situation), he strikes matches for his cigarettes on, among other things, a whore's bustier, a lynched man's boot, the back of a businessman's hat and a bandit's toothy grin. Nero had made three Westerns between *Django* and *A Professional Gun* (*Texas Adios* (1966), *Massacre Time* (1966), *Man, Pride, Vengeance* (1967)) as well as an aborted attempt at cracking Hollywood with the Lancelot role in the musical *Camelot* (1967), but *A Professional Gun* gave him his best Western role and was a box office smash. It was also Corbucci's most successful Western in the States when it was released there by United Artists in 1970 (under the title *The Mercenary*).

Musante is good as Paco (a variation on Tomas Milian's Cuchillo character from Sollima's films), but it is Palance, as Curly, the black-suited, carnation-wearing homosexual hired gun and saloon owner, who steals the show. Palance did some of his best work in Europe and was always good in Spaghettis, enlivening even the weakest efforts, but for Corbucci (here and in *Compañeros*) he gave superbly unhinged performances. Early in *A Professional Gun* he politely asks one of his own hit men (who has just bungled a job) if he's married or has kids (he has neither), before having him pitchforked to death. Later Curly's stripped by Paco's men and left naked in the desert, miles from civilisation, but when he finally catches up with Paco (who's hiding out in a rodeo show), their gundown in a bullring recalls the climax of *For A Few Dollars More*. Paco (in a clown costume) faces Curly, while the Polak acts as referee. When the shots are fired we think Curly has survived, until blood begins to drip from his carnation and he crumples into the dust. Curly's penchant for crossing himself (like

Tuco in *The Good, The Bad And The Ugly*) is offset by his ruthless methods. In one scene he questions a wounded bandit as to Paco's whereabouts. When no help is forthcoming, he puts a grenade in the bandit's mouth, pulls the pin and makes a swift exit.

The Verdict: Undoubtedly Corbucci's most polished Western, this movie was the perfect blend of explosive action and revolutionary rhetoric. 4/5

The Price Of Power (1969)

Director Tonino Valerii

Cast: Giuliano Gemma (Bill), Van Johnson (President Garfield), Warren Vanders (MacDonald) 108 minutes

Story: In 1880, the anti-slavery Northern President James A Garfield travels to Dallas, Texas, to make a political address concerning his reforms. But though the Civil War ended a long time ago, the city is still run by corrupt Southern politicians, bankers, lawmen and lawyers who, in league with a gang of bandits, want the President dead. When he arrives, the President is assassinated by the corrupt Sheriff's men and an innocent Negro is framed for the crime. The corrupt Southerners plan to blackmail the new President with certain incriminating documents. Yankee gunman Bill Willer's father has also been killed by the rebels (he knew of the assassination plot) and so Willer, with the help of Garfield's aide, MacDonald, sets about destroying the Confederate gang. The Negro knows who really killed Garfield and is shot as he is being taken to Fort Worth for trial, but Willer and MacDonald defeat the villains. Willer gets hold of the inflammatory documents, but realises how important they are and allows MacDonald to return them to Washington - the South won't rise again.

Background: Valerii's third Western was also his most political. Also known as *Texas* and *The Death Of A President*, *The Price Of Power* was that rarest of Spaghetti Westerns - one that's based on historical fact. As anyone with the vaguest knowledge of American history can see, this is a thinly-disguised reworking of the assassination of John F Kennedy in Dallas by persons unknown. In macabre echoes of that fateful day in November 1963 Valerii's film appropriates various factual details and weaves them into his scenario. The President's tour of Dallas in an opened-topped carriage recalls Kennedy's limousine ride, while other aspects are even more explicit - the human rights issues (as relevant as ever), the killing of a 'patsy' between jails, a phoney Warren Commission-like inquiry, the shooting from an overpass (instead of the Grassy Knoll) during a cavalcade around Dallas and the President's wife's pink dress (just like Jackie Kennedy's) splattered with the President's blood.

But the real cleverness of *The Price Of Power* is the effortlessness with which Valerii adopts these details and issues effectively to a Western setting. The film is not without its faults (the inquest scenes tend to drag and the plot gets a little convoluted) and certain aspects are clearly Spaghetti-esque (various prolonged stylised duels and a crippled newspaperman with a rifle hidden in his crutch), but in the main it sustains its tension throughout. The politicising is cleverly handled and the film is truly epic in scope - Valerii's equivalent of *Once Upon A Time In The West* (which used the same town and ranch sets). The clandestine Southern group responsible for organising the assassination have all the classic 'corrupt' ingredients - a deceitful banker, a racist governor, a blackmailed Vice President, a crooked attorney and a conniving sheriff. Like Valerii's other movies, *Day Of Anger* and *My Name Is Nobody*, the dignitaries are mixed up with outlaws.

Gemma, better known for his Ringo movies (and Valerii's previous film *Day Of Anger*) gives one of his best performances. It's his last great Western before he turned to comedy in the wake of the Trinity movies. Van Johnson, an American expat is excellent as the President, Fernando Rey (later of the *French Connection* movies) is effective as a crooked banker and leader of the insurrectionists, while Warren Vanders is suitably ambivalent as the FBI agent who teams up with Gemma. In one memorable scene the idealistic Northern President states his belief that no bullet can stop an idea. Willer is more realistic and replies that the only thing that counts in Dallas is the Colt. It can stop anything, "Even a President."

The Verdict: A fusion of themes from earlier Reconstruction Era Spaghettis (*The Tramplers*, *The Hellbenders*) and the Kennedy Conspiracy results in Valerii's most original film. In a humorous detail, one of the buildings in Valerii's Dallas even resembles the Texas School Book Depository, with its distinctive high arched windows. But James Garfield was assassinated in 1881 (not 1880), shot in the back by a insane young man who failed in his application to get on the federal government payroll. Such is Spaghetti Western artistic licence. 3/5

Sabata (1969)

Director Gianfranco Parolini

Cast: Lee Van Cleef (Sabata), William Berger (Banjo), Franco Ressel (Stengel), Pedro Sanchez (Carrincha) 102 minutes

Story: A shipment of army cash is stolen from the bank in Daugherty. A mysterious stranger named Sabata recovers the money and is rewarded by the army, but it soon becomes apparent that the men really responsible for the heist were three respectable townsmen - the judge, the saloon-keeper and Stengel a rancher. Sabata, with the aid of a Mexican drunkard called Carrincha and a drifter called Banjo (who lives with Jane, a saloon girl), sets about blackmailing the trio, promising to tell the authorities if their demands aren't met. Stengel employs various gunmen to kill Sabata, but he seems indestructible. Eventually, Stengel hires Banjo to turn traitor, but even this ruse fails. Sabata, Carrincha and an acrobatic Indian named Alley Cat attack Stengel's ranch and decimate his gang. During the battle Sabata kills the saloon-keeper and Stengel, but Banjo takes the Judge prisoner. Banjo faces Sabata in a gunfight 'bet' (bankrolled by the judge) and kills Sabata. Leaving town with his winnings for nailing Sabata, Banjo takes Sabata's corpse for burial, but in a final twist Sabata's still alive. He takes Banjo's haul, splits it with Carrincha and Alley Cat and scatters Banjo's share to the wind, leaving his ex-partner the unenviable task of collecting it.

Background: This is Parolini's most famous and lucrative Western. He had been making films since the late fifties and they nearly all feature acrobats, making his action sequences more impressive than most Italian movies. The year before he made *Sabata*, Parolini (under the pseudonym 'Frank Kramer') helmed *Five For Hell*, a *Dirty Dozen* variant with Klaus Kinski as an SS officer, and *Sartana* (full title *If You Meet Sartana, Pray For Your Death*), which was essentially a dry run for this movie - Berger even played the second lead. For the title role, Parolini axed Gianni Garko (who had played Sartana, and would again for the next four years) and cast Van Cleef. Van Cleef's character was based almost entirely on his role as Colonel Mortimer in *For A Few Dollars More*. Instead of a Colonel, Sabata is an ex-Confederate Major and instead of the gimmicks Mortimer was armed with (a derringer, his arsenal and his long-barrelled pistol) Sabata has a long-range rifle and a customised derringer (that has barrels in the handle). He was also dressed in Mortimer's trademark black suit and frock coat. Banjo, his partner, has a Winchester hidden in a banjo, Carrincha is a knife-thrower and the Indian Alley Cat is an acrobat. Even the villain, Stengel, has a deadly cane that fires metal spikes. This inventiveness makes up for what the film lacks in plot, which for the most part consists of elaborately staged shoot-outs, as Sabata continually outwits his opponents.

The opening heist is beautifully concise. The robbery is carried out by a group of Stengel's men in league with a troupe of villainous acrobats, who employ a seesaw to gain access to the bank and then dispatch the safe onto a wagon along a set of portable railroad tracks. True enough, this sounds ridiculous, but by 1969 Spaghettis were getting pretty thin on imagination. Parolini's acrobatic injections had already worked very well in the muscleman spectacular, the war movie and the world of super-agents. It was only natural for him to apply his outrageous style to Westerns. The plot is also particularly clever. Instead of the usual plotline of a hero tracking down the bank robbers, Sabata has shot and captured the perpetrators in the opening 15 minutes. The three businessmen behind the heist take fright and eliminate anyone else involved in the robbery (a Mafia-esque ploy), leaving Sabata the task of blackmailing the trio with the knowledge that they are responsible - thereby lining his own pocket. The ambiguous Banjo sides with Sabata, but eventually sells him out, while Sabata's two compadres - the fat Mexican layabout and the acrobatic Indian - form a 'Magnificent Three' against Stengel's huge gang. In the beautifully-organised finale, with the air thick with dynamite and bullets, they cut a swathe through Stengel's camp, dispensing revenge from a mining car on tracks. Marcello Giombini's humorous score (especially the lively opening song) contributed to the film's huge success which reaffirmed Van Cleef's box-office clout. So much so that it started an acrobatic sub-genre, including Parolini's *The Bounty Hunters* (1970, aka *Adios Sabata*) and *The Return Of Sabata* (1971), which was set in a circus, for once providing a reason why so many acrobats were hanging around town.

The Verdict: A greatly entertaining Western and the last decent Spaghetti before the Trinity-style comedies revamped the genre the following year. Worth seeing for the wonderful moment when Banjo strides into the main street to face a gang out for vengeance, with only his banjo for company. 4/5

End Of The Trail: 1970-76

Compañeros (1970)

Director Sergio Corbucci

Cast: Franco Nero (Yod Peterson), Tomas Milian (Vasco), Fernando Rey (Xantos), Jack Palance (John), Jose Bodalo (Mongo) 117 minutes

Story: Yod Peterson, a Swedish mercenary and arms dealer, arrives in the Mexican town of San Bernardino. The settlement is in the throes of the Mexican Revolution as two factions fight it out - the Mexican rebels under General Mongo and the largely pacifist Xantistas, the followers of a local hero, Professor Xantos. The safe in town has a fortune inside, but no one knows the combination except Xantos - and he's a political prisoner of the Americans across the border in Yuma. Mongo sends Yod and Vasco (one of the General's brigands) on a mission to rescue the professor. After many explosive adventures they return with Xantos, but Mongo captures the Xantistas and threatens to murder them if Xantos doesn't surrender. With the contents of the safe at stake, Yod and Vasco (who has been converted to Xantos' cause) take on Mongo's army and defeat it, at the cost of Xantos' life. But the safe didn't hold a fortune, just the true wealth of the community - a few ears of corn. As Yod prepares to leave town, Vasco urges the Swede to stay. With the counter-revolutionary army on the way, Yod decides to join the revolutionaries in the imminent battle.

Background: Cut from the same cloth as the hugely successful *A Professional Gun,* and often touted as its sequel, *Compañeros* is a more elaborate, excessive remake - as though Corbucci couldn't fit all his imaginative ideas into the first film and made this to use them up. The central axis of *Compañeros* is again a relationship between a European mercenary (this time Swedish) and a Mexican revolutionary (highlighting all the familiar political and cultural differences), but although the Mexican (like Paco Roman in *A Professional Gun*) gains a conscience, this time the soldier of fortune also has a change of heart and sides with the rebels in the finale. Nero again played the mercenary (Yod, christened 'The Penguin' by Vasco, due to his gaiters and tailcoat) with his customary cool, while Milian played Vasco as a cross between Cuchillo (his peasant persona from Sollima's Westerns) and Cuban icon Che Guevara (Milian is actually a Cuban). In the effective prologue, Vasco is the servant of a Federale general, polishing his boots, until Mongo's men arrive and massacre the government troops. Thereafter, he polishes Mongo's

70

boots - such is Vasco's lot. Whoever wins the revolution, the poor will always lose.

Palance, cast as John, a villainous gringo (this time a mercenary and Yod's ex-partner) is again the most excessive character in the film - swathed in a black cloak, addicted to marijuana and with a pet falcon named Marsha perched on his wooden hand. John lost his hand when Yod abandoned him during a previous adventure and John was caught and nailed to a tree - it was Marsha who ate his hand to free him. Now John wants revenge and doggedly shadows the Swede throughout the movie.

In a recent interview, Palance was asked why such a fine actor as himself had never won an Oscar before 1991, to which he incredulously replied, "What? In Spaghetti Westerns?", though he immensely enjoyed making them, and Europe made him rich when Hollywood had forgotten him. *Compañeros*, at nearly two hours, is dreadfully overlong and there is much talk about revolution and pacifism on the journey back from Yuma, which jars with the action sequences (though there's plenty of those too, involving dynamite and machine-guns). In one excellent scene, Vasco and Yod escape in an old army lorry, pursued by the cavalry, until the steering wheel comes off in Vasco's hands and they end up in a river. There are a couple of significant female roles in the movie (a Xantista named Lola who ends up marrying Vasco, and Zaira, one of Yod's old flames), but their characters are uncharacteristically sketchy - most unusual for a Corbucci Western.

Compañeros is worth seeing for one reason however - the crackerjack finale. Though *A Professional Gun* is a better film, *Compañeros'* climax is the highlight of the movie. Xantos walks alone into San Bernardino to give himself up. Realising that Mongo will shoot the professor on sight (and his pacifist followers won't lift a finger to help), Yod rides into town to face Mongo, John and the bandits. On a par with Peckinpah's Battle Of Bloody Porch from *The Wild Bunch* (without the slow-mo effects) Yod levels the entire gang with Winchester, pistol and machine-gun, as Morricone's up-tempo chaotic title song 'Vamos A Matar Compañeros!' (Let's Go Kill, Comrades! - lyrics written by Corbucci himself) blares on the soundtrack. As with all Corbucci's Westerns, there's a sting in the tail - here the safe contains only ears of corn and a sickle, the only wealth the peasants possess. The last of Corbucci's Revolution trilogy, *What Am I Doing In The Middle Of A Revolution?* (1972) again saw two characters (an Italian thespian and a priest) caught up in the conflict, with less success, though it did raise some interesting points about the Catholic church, and the relationship between the fantasy and reality of an Italian Western (with Italian actors playing Italian actors having adventures down Mexico way). It also included some good moments: a daring rescue from a firing squad with a length of rope dangling from a biplane; a motorbike and side-car chase; a parody of the crop-duster sequence from *North By Northwest* (1959); and, in one of Corbucci's weirdest ideas, a band of one-handed machete-wielding revolutionaries who wear skeleton masks as they get revenge on their oppressors.

The Verdict: Compañeros, though still a cut above its equally light-hearted imitators like *Long Live Your Death* (1971) and *Heads I Kill You Tails You Die* (1971), is not as good a film as it thinks it is. It has a great (and largely undeserved) reputation on the continent as one of the classic Spaghettis, mostly because of three star turns (Nero, Palance and Milian) at their peak of popularity. However, the film didn't fair as well as *A Professional Gun* in the US when it was released (cut) in 1971. 3/5

A Man Called Sledge (1970)

Director Vic Morrow

Cast: James Garner (Sledge), Dennis Weaver (Ward), Claude Akins (Hooker), John Marley (Old Man), Laura Antonelli (Maria) 88 minutes

Story: Following a bungled stagecoach hold-up, outlaw Sledge hooks up with his gang in Rockville. There he learns from an old man, an ex-convict, that there's a million in gold deposited in a cell in maximum security, so Sledge sets about stealing it. Realising that when in transit the shipment is heavily guarded by 40 army riders armed to the teeth and a Gatling gun, Sledge decides to take the gold from the inside - he and his cohort Ward (disguised as a Sheriff) get themselves arrested and deposited in maximum security, in a cell next to the cache. They manage to break out, free all the prisoners and make off with the gold with the gang, but Ward is killed in the confusion. Hiding in the desert with their haul, the bandits split the gold, but squabble over the proceeds. One of the gang is killed in an argument and Sledge makes off with the lot. He heads for the town of Siego to meet his girl Maria, but the gang, now led by the old man, have got there first. Maria is killed and they steal the gold from Sledge and hide it. In the action, Sledge gets his arm crippled, but he manages to take on the gang and defeat them - even though he doesn't know where the gold is hidden.

Background: The film opens beautifully in a *Big Silence*-esque snow-bound landscape for the failed stage robbery, but although Garner's hero is called Sledge the action soon shifts to more familiar Spaghetti territory - the starkness of the desert. Like Clint Eastwood, James Coburn, Ty Hardin and Burt Reynolds, Garner was a popular leading man in the sixties who started in TV Westerns, made it to bigger-budget roles and dabbled in Italian Westerns. Here he's cast as Sledge, an outlaw who'll stop at nothing to get his hands on a gold shipment - risking the lives of his closest friends and even his girl. Needless to say, in the pessimistic Spaghetti West, Garner loses all. His role is completely atypical. Garner had played Brett Maverick on TV and later sent-up Westerns with *Support Your Local Sheriff* (1968) and the sequel *Support Your Local Local Gunfighter* (1971). He'd also turned in hardman performances in *Duel At Diablo* (1966) and *Hour Of The Gun* (1967), but this is his only outright anti-heroic role - a charismatic persona edged with bitterness.

Like *The Hills Run Red* (1966) and *Dead Or Alive* (1967), *A Man Called Sledge* uses several well-known American actors in supporting roles as Sledge's gang, including Weaver, later the hapless protagonist of Spielberg's *Duel* (1977), Akins (a fifties B-Western stalwart) and Marley, who played the producer who finds his favourite horse's severed head in bed with him in *The Godfather* (1972). In complete contrast, the female lead Antonelli later became a well-known actress in Italian porn movies (though her nude scenes in *A Man Called Sledge* were removed from the English print).

This is a very well made, cleverly plotted movie. Director Morrow elicits maximum tension from the hero's incarceration in the moonlit, hellish prison, where inmates howl at the moon like werewolves and the warders goad them on. The central theme - both narratively and visually - is that the West is a card game that you always lose. In the snow, after the stage robbery (where an innocent bystander catches a stray bullet), Sledge and his partner Mallory shelter in a saloon. Mallory gets involved in a poker game and is killed after he wins the pot. Later, after the prison break, the gang hole up in some ruins in the desert. A card game ensues and one of the gang is killed by the old man for cheating (refilling his gold sack with sand). Sledge, disgusted, resolves to clean the old man out. In a superbly-shot montage, Sledge deals cards in slow motion, flicking them spinning into the air, as he wins the game. This 'West as poker' theme is even echoed in Gianni Ferrio's excellent title song 'Other Men's Gold' ('Beware my friend, of the curse that follows other men's gold') and in the eccentric score. Even after succeeding in the heist and winning at cards, Sledge still loses the game…and the gold.

But it's with the finale that the film gels and veers into really interesting territory as it examines the relationship between greed, religion and love, and how they're bound together by violence. Sledge arrives in Siego as a black-shrouded, candle-bearing religious procession makes its way through town. While they're away at the ritual, the town is deserted, a silent battleground for Sledge and his ex-comrades. One manages to put a knife through Sledge's forearm, rendering it useless, so he binds a crucifix to his arm as a makeshift splint. His girlfriend is raped and murdered in a church and he manages to kill his former partners, even though he hasn't learnt the gold's hiding place. The final image is particularly powerful. As Sledge leaves town he passes a sea of holy candles and prayer lanterns, and then rides alone into the desert.

The Verdict: Though some of the Americans seem a little lost in Almeria and the script is sometimes overly clichéd, this is a good solid Western. The opening and planning scenes are exciting, the heist suspenseful, the dénouement brutally ironic. What more do you want? 3/5

They Call Me Trinity (1970)

Director Enzo Barboni

Cast: Terence Hill (Trinity), Bud Spencer (Bambino), Farley Granger (Major Harrison), Steffen Zacharias (Jonathan) 105 minutes

Story: Good-for-nothing layabout gunslinger Trinity arrives in town and discovers his horse-thieving half-brother Bambino masquerading as the Sheriff. The town is run by a corrupt rancher, Major Harrison, who is intent on ridding a fertile valley of the bunch of Mormons who've settled there - he wants to use the land to graze his horse herd. To get rid of them, the Major recruits a vicious but bumbling Mexican bandit and his moronic gang. Bambino makes Trinity his deputy and the two decide to help the Mormons out, but the more Trinity interferes in the Major's plans, the more determined the rancher is to get rid of the settlement. Trinity falls for two of the Mormon girls (polygamy is permitted in Mormon circles) and thinks about settling down, but the Major forces a confrontation. Lacking any weapons, Trinity and Bambino improvise and tutor the Mormon pacifists how to brawl, while rustler Bambino has his eyes on the Major's horse herd. In the massed fist fight that follows, the brothers and the Mormons teach the Major a much-needed lesson. But Trinity lets the Mormons have the Major's horses, thereby ruining the rustling scheme and Bambino leaves in disgust, soon to be followed by Trinity, when he realises that he isn't cut out for a life of hard toil and prayer.

Background: An outstanding comedy Western and the best of the comedy Spaghettis that swamped Europe in the final, highly successful phase of the Italian Western boom. Funny from start to finish and entertainingly action-packed along the way, this made Hill and Spencer superstars as

Europe's answer to Stan Laurel and Oliver Hardy. Early in his career, Hardy was nicknamed 'Baby' Hardy, which perhaps influenced Barboni when he chose the name Bambino for Spencer's bearlike, bearded man-mountain - great in a fist fight but not the sharpest knife in the drawer. Hill, as Trinity (or 'The Right Hand Of the Devil' as he's referred to throughout, Bambino's 'The Left') is the most appealing and easygoing gunslinger of the whole Spaghetti genre. Caked in a layer of dust, he wears his gunbelt slung so low he can barely reach it and travels around on an Indian horse-drawn travois. But he's certainly quick on the draw and the speeded-up action gives a surreal edge to the comedy set pieces. Unlike later comedy Spaghettis, Barboni doesn't overdo these effects, the extended mass brawl finale being the only exception. Moreover, many of the Trinity derivatives lost their effectiveness when they opted for abso-lutely no fatalities (in this film there are some casualties) in a bid to reach a younger audience.

Barboni had long wanted to make a comedy Western and had been touting the Trinity script for years. He started as a cinematographer and worked extensively for Corbucci and others, photographing both the good and the bad of the genre including *Django*, *Texas Adios, The Hellbenders*, *Rita Of The West*, *Django Get A Coffin Ready* and *The Five Man Army*. He began directing in 1969 with the awful Western *Chuck Mool* (also called *The Unholy Four*) and adopted the pseudonym E B Clucher, a name he stuck with throughout his career. *They Call Me Trinity* was his break-through and was just what the Spaghetti Western needed, because the genre had died on its feet. Though these movies are generally referred to as Slapstick Spaghettis, this first entry is more concerned with parodying Westerns (especially Leone's movies and *The Magnificent Seven*) and concentrating on clever verbal humour, rather than the outright fists-fests that later entries became. Much of the humour is pretty unsophisticated - especially the belching and disgusting eating habits that also became sig-natures of these Spaghetti comedies, though *Trinity* is reasonably restrained in this respect. Barboni's reverential humour is noticeable in the film's opening sequence. Trinity arrives at a stagecoach station by travois - like Laurel and Hardy arrive in Brushwood Gulch at the beginning of *Way Out West* (1937) - and encounters two bounty hunters. They ask his name and the hero answers, "They call me Trinity". "They say you've got the fastest gun around", ventures one bounty hunter. "Is that what they say?" smiles Trinity, "Gees." Trinity's lazy, self-effacing manner endeared him to audiences and handsome, blue-eyed Hill's performance is his best. Equally so, the film wouldn't have worked without surly Spencer who plays every scene as though he's been woken up in the middle of his nap and lets out a bored sigh before beating the hell out of the Major's men. But both Hill and Spencer also display superb comic timing. At one point, Bambino receives a letter from the Sheriff he ambushed (and stole the star from), asking for his help. "Now he wants me to give him a hand to find me", deadpans Bambino. When the duo visit the Mormon camp for the first time, one of the brethren hollers, "Welcome brothers". Bambino turns to Trinity and asks, "Who told him we were brothers?" The humour is a little rougher and much cleverer than later, more juvenile Hill and Spencer entries. They perform an impromptu operation on a Mexican prisoner, Trinity sticking his finger in the wound, to plug up the hole. Because of their zeal with the anaesthetic (a bottle of whiskey) the Mexican winds up an alcoholic. And when Trinity becomes deputy and sets about teaching the Major a lesson, his efforts aren't appreciated by his brother - "One store destroyed, three heads split like overripe melons, one man wounded and one castrated. All in two hours, just two hours I left you alone".

The villain, dapper Major Harrison, is portrayed by Farley Granger - better known for his performances in Hitchcock's *Rope* (1948) and *Strangers On A Train* (1951). Granger plays the Major as a genteel Southern 'genulmun', but it's the supporting cast that added so much to the movie. Zacharias plays the Sheriff's housekeeper Jonathan Swift, who constantly bemoans Bambino's ineffectual peacekeeping. Every time something happens in town, the lawman is somewhere else - "I've never met such an unlucky Sheriff." And his description of the real Sheriff on Bambino's trail is wittily understated, "Moustache, star on his chest, crutches. A typical crippled Sheriff, looking for the fellows that made him that way." The Mexican bandit gang hired by the Major are a comic version of Leone's renegades, with their evil laughter stretched to extremes and a bizarre code of honour. Their payment for getting rid of the Mormons is to receive a share of the Major's horses, but the bandits would prefer it if they were allowed to 'steal' the steeds - to work for pay is too embarrassing. And nothing in Barboni's West is sacred, as the numerous gags at the Mormons' expense, the parody title song and imaginative whistled score (by Franco Micalizzi) attest.

The Verdict: Easily the best of the comic Spaghettis, this film is the funniest (and most overlooked) comedy Western prior to Mel Brooks' *Blazing Saddles* (1973). Though Hill and Spencer's finest hour and three quarters, it also sounded the death knell for Spaghetti Westerns. Judging by the quality of seventies Spaghettis it was a pretty fair swap. 5/5

Blindman (1971)

Director Ferdinando Baldi

Cast: Tony Anthony (Blindman), Lloyd Battista (Domingo), Ringo Starr (Candy), Raf Baldassare (General), Magna Konopka (Sweet Mama) 101 minutes

Story: A blind gunslinger is hired to escort 50 mail-order brides to a mining camp in Texas. But when he arrives to pick up his charges, he finds that the women have been kidnapped by a Mexican bandit, Domingo, his brother Candy and their gang of cut-throats, to be employed as whores for the Mexican Army in a bordello run by the bandits' sister Sweet Mama. After much double-crossing, the Blindman, with the aid of a Mexican General, manages to recover the brides, but the General steals them, leaving the Blindman no choice but to set off in pursuit.

Background: It should be said from the off that this is a particularly exploitative and misogynist film, especially in the amount of nudity included (which is unusual for Spaghettis) and the violence meted out on the 50 women. That said, the film was massively popular worldwide on its original release - everywhere except Britain and the States. *Blindman* is one of a series of Spaghettis that included disabled or physically-impaired characters. There was a Fellini-esque profusion of epileptics, amputees, cripples and dwarfs in Spaghettis ranging from *Dead Or Alive* and *The Price Of Power* to *The Good, The Bad And The Ugly* and *A Professional Gun.* In *Deaf Smith & Johnny Ears* (1972) Anthony Quinn played a deaf-mute gunslinger and *The Big Silence*'s hero is also a mute. Moreover many Spaghetti heroes end up incapacitated by the final duel, but *Blindman* approaches its subject as an outlandish parody - the whole idea of a blind shootist surviving one gunfight, let alone an entire film, is ridiculous from the off.

After the Stranger trilogy, Anthony wrote and starred in this movie, which is his best. Though it is a highly imaginative and darkly humorous tale of revenge, with much quasi-religious rhetoric, the film is best remembered for the performance by The Beatles ex-drummer, Ringo Starr. The film was produced by Allen Klein (who from 1969 was their manager), who also made a cameo appearance in the film along with erst-while Beatles assistant Mal Evans. Starr's performance is one of many film roles in the seventies (after The Beatles split up) and he acquits him-self very well as a vicious bandit called Candy. In one of the strangest scenes in the film, he is killed, but his brother still wants him to go through with his wedding to a Mexican girl, so the ceremony goes ahead, with the girl in full wedding regalia and Candy in an open-topped coffin.

But it is Anthony as the philosophical blind stranger who really makes an impact. Dressed in a battered patchwork duster (with one sleeve missing) and an outsized floppy sombrero, he uses his Winchester as a makeshift white cane. And when he faces his enemies, he aims for the sounds they make (cocked guns, coughing, laughing) in an idea borrowed from Corbucci's *Minnesota Clay* (1964). When the Blindman captures Candy he drapes the bandit in cowbells, so he can't make a move without making a sound. In a nice touch, the Blindman is led around by his horse (christened Boss), who is as helpful and watchful as any sidekick - he even comes to his master's whistle. But the Blindman is treated very badly throughout - no quarter is given by his adversaries for the fact that he's blind. He is badly beaten, is served a snake in a salad (a really suspenseful moment) and in the end is duped by the Mexican General, who gags the mail-order brides and makes off with them. Earlier, the General evens up the final gunfight by burning bandit Domingo's eyes out with a cigar. Anthony himself suffered terribly during filming. He wore blue contact lenses for the role, but the sand and dust kept getting under the lenses and made filming hell.

Even though the brides are treated badly throughout the movie, they are undoubtedly an excellent aspect of the story. In an astounding action sequence the women (all in white dresses) make a bid for freedom en masse, loaded onto two carts, but the bandits catch up with them (the wagons get stuck in the sand) and the women make a bolt for it on foot, with brutal results. The final gundown in the graveyard which parodies *The Good, The Bad And The Ugly* is also effective and much of the film's success is down to composer Stelvio Cipriani, who contributes his best Western score - an evocative blend of chants, shrieks, sitars and guitars that recalls Morricone's scores for *The Big Silence*, *The Good, The Bad And The Ugly* and the Sci-Fi movie *Danger: Diabolik* (1968).

The Verdict: This is an exploitation movie through and through (some of the sequences look like they belong in a women's chain gang movie like *Sweet Sugar*), but if you ignore the film's dodgy moral stance vis-à-vis the female characters then it's really an entertainingly refreshing Western. Well worth seeing. 3/5

Duck You Sucker (1971)

Director Sergio Leone

Cast: Rod Steiger (Juan), James Coburn (Mallory), Romolo Valli (Dr Villega) 152 minutes

Story: During the Mexican Revolution, Juan (an illiterate Mexican bandit) and his sons are planning to rob the bank at Mesa Verde. On the way they encounter an Irish dynamiter, Sean Mallory, an ex-IRA terrorist on the run from the authorities. Together they blow up the bank, but unbeknownst to Juan, it is being used as a political prison and Juan is instantly a revolutionary hero. Mallory is working for the rebels, led by Dr Villega, but the rebellion's success leads to government reprisals, under the vicious Colonel Gunther Ruiz. The revolutionary army split up and Mallory and Juan manage to stall the army's advance during an ambush at a bridge, but elsewhere Juan's sons are trapped and killed and Villega is tortured into betraying many key figures in his organisation. Eventually the rebels decide to stop and fight and ambush the army's train. In a pitched battle Ruiz is killed and Mallory is badly wounded and while Juan goes for help he commits suicide by blowing himself up.

Background: Along with his decade-spanning gangster monolith *Once Upon A Time In America* (1984), this is arguably Leone's weakest film and certainly a poor attempt at a Political Spaghetti Western. This is even more obvious when compared to similar films by Corbucci, Sollima and Damiani (films that centre on the uneasy alliance between a Mexican peasant and a foreigner - often a mercenary). Leone's film can't make up its mind whether it has a serious political dynamic (à la *A Bullet For The General* or *The Big Gundown*) or a jokier, more parodic atmosphere (like *A Professional Gun*). The writers involved in some of these movies (Sergio Donati, Luciano Vincenzoni) contributed to *Duck You Sucker*. Though the political message is as powerful as any of the above, Leone's film is overlong, ponderous and overblown, and includes too much physical, crude and downright distasteful humour (an unsavoury and unwelcome addition to mainstream Italian cinema in the seventies) and a plethora of bad language that seems at odds with the lyrical elements of the story. Steiger is allowed to overact outrageously. Not in the entertaining way that Eli Wallach livened up *The Good, The Bad And The Ugly*, but in a ham-fisted, bullish way that ensures that he's always centre stage - again proving that he can wave his arms about, adopt a funny accent and shout louder than anyone else.

By contrast, Coburn, the original choice for the hero of *A Fistful Of Dollars*, gives one of the best performances of his career - he's certainly never been better. He is also the best equipped and most emotionally wracked of the mercenaries who found themselves in the Spaghetti West's version of the Mexican Revolution. His first appearance in the film is one of the high spots. A huge explosion stops Juan and his gang in their tracks. Through the smoke and dust appears a motorcycle, the rider kitted out in goggles and leather helmet (like a WW1 flying ace). Later when Mallory unbuttons his long duster coat, it is lined with sticks of dynamite and fuses, while his flask carries a vial of nitroglycerine. Juan soon surmises that Mallory is a handy ally to have when robbing a bank - in fact he imagines a halo above Saint Sean's head and later refers to the nitro as Holy Water. But for every finely-observed detail and superbly-executed action sequence, there's a scene that goes on for far too long or a rant from Steiger, to completely ruin the pace.

With *Once Upon A Time In The West* Leone had set himself apart from the compatriot directors. Even the biggest-budget Spaghettis couldn't match the grandeur of his movies after *The Good, The Bad And The Ugly*, but in many cases a lower-budget approach made the other movies more interesting. Big sets, big-name stars and big explosions don't always make a better film. *Duck You Sucker* often looks more like a Peckinpah movie (a director originally asked to direct the project) and also like the star-laden super-productions set in Mexico, like *Villa Rides* (1968), *100 Rifles* (1968) and *Two Mules For Sister Sara* (1970), films that existed solely for their action sequences, with no thought behind them. Moreover, when Leone started out in Westerns in 1964 he wanted to rip all the superfluous talking out of the Western and go back to a more primitive world, where guns spoke more than badly-dubbed words. After his radical approach, bringing so much life, modernism and beauty to the genre, it was ironic that his last Western and his gangster epic were longwinded affairs that verged on the boring. But the film does have some tremendous redeeming features which make it worth watching. Mallory's flashbacks to his time in the IRA in Dublin have a lyricism absent in the rest of the movie and Ennio Morricone's majestic (and in some moments downright surreal) score is far superior to the images it accompanies. The main theme has a superb soprano vocal and swathes of strings, a more up-tempo of his famous theme from *Once Upon A Time In The West*. International distributors edited the movie, and subsequent releases have similarly exorcised much of the bad language and trimmed the film, though a full version is now available. It was also released under the titles *A Fistful Of Dynamite* and *Once Upon A Time In The Revolution*, but that didn't change the film's fortunes - it didn't gross anywhere near as well as the Dollars trilogy. The scenes where Mallory and Juan first meet, and the bridge demolition (a spectacular action sequence which is Leone at his best) are the film's finest moments. The protagonist's central relationship has been dealt with better by other directors, while the train collision climax falls flat because the engines look suspiciously like models (which is what they are).

The Verdict: The full version of *Sucker* is better for being longer (the early sections of the film make more sense), and is obviously the second part of Leone's next trilogy. A 'Birth Of A Nation' scenario that spans the coming of the railroads, the emergence of big business, the death of the cowboy and the appearance of gangsters. According to Mallory's motto in the movie 'Revolution means confusion' and on that score Leone has aptly captured the flavour of the period. 3/5

Trinity Is Still My Name (1971)

Director Enzo Barboni

Cast: Terence Hill (Trinity), Bud Spencer (Bambino), Yanti Somer (Wendy), Harry Carey Jnr. (Trinity's father), Jessica Dublin (Trinity's mother) 115 minutes

Story: After completely failing in a horse rustling scheme, Trinity and Bambino team up again and turn their hands to outlawry, but in their first attempted robbery they find themselves giving their victims money. Arriving in Tescosa they are mistaken for Federal Agents sent to investigate the criminal activities of Parker, a wealthy rancher. Bought off by the villain to turn a blind eye, Trinity discovers that Parker is making a fortune running guns from San Jose and selling them to roving Mexican bandit gangs. The whole plot is hidden in a mission, with the innocent monks forced to front the operation. The duo eventually save the monks, expose the operation, defeat Parker's gang and confiscate the proceeds, only to have to hand it over when a Texas Ranger suspects that he's seen Bambino's face on a reward poster.

Background: This is the second Trinity film and the last to star Hill and Spencer as the ill-matched, hard-hitting, fast-drawing duo. It is also still one of the most successful Italian films ever made. This time around, the action includes gun-running monks, crooked ranchers, farting babies and even a guest appearance by the heroes' parents. Less well-structured than *They Call Me Trinity*, this is nevertheless a superior comedy Western. Instead of the quick-fire, punchy format of the first movie, director Barboni (again signing himself E B Clucher) stretches the scenes out much longer, so that the film becomes a series of 10-minute sketches, each strung around a comic Western situation (a card game, a confrontation in a saloon or a meal in a fancy French restaurant). The shoot-outs are much more imaginative, with Trinity's quick-draw further quickened by speeding up the footage. In one scene, he has time to slap his opponent across the face before drawing his own gun (these rapid comic effects reappeared to lesser effect in *My Name Is Nobody*) and his adversaries are gunslingers with parodic names like Stinger Eastsmith and Wildcard Hendricks.

The fist fights are similarly impressive, with the tight choreography making the action both brutal (in a *Tom And Jerry* kind of way) and funny, as stuntmen fly through the air, get hit by highly unconvincing breakaway furniture or wind up on the receiving end of one of Bambino's pile-driving punches - Trinity tends to hit a couple of adversaries to show willing and then leave it to his brother.

As with the previous Trinity film, there is some messy eating accompanied by farting and belching, but in this movie it's raised to an art form. A running gag features a family of settlers with a baby called Little Ebaneezer, who has a noisy problem with wind (or 'aerodogy' as it's diagnosed in the movie), much to Bambino's amusement. And the film has two set pieces that rely on the heroes disgusting table manners for laughs. In the first, the duo share a meal with their parents that consists of some kind of roast bird - their mother can't identify what species, but she caught it hanging around the ranch. In the second, the most notorious and riotous sequence in the film, Trinity and Bambino, now dressed in smart suits and bowler-hats (which they bought with their winnings from a poker game) decide to eat out in a fancy French restaurant. Not having a clue how to eat in such a posh establishment, they drive the Maitre D' and his put-upon assistant Jorge to distraction, offend their fellow diners, go for their guns when a waiter pops a cork and douse a Flambé dish.

Barboni must have got a big laugh out of casting one of John Ford's favourite actors Harry Carey Jnr. (in his first Spaghetti Western) as Trinity's father. His speech to his two sons - trying to get them to embark on a life of crime, so that he can be proud of the prices on their heads - is played for laughs. In more serious movies it would have been a heartfelt plea to settle down. But there is less of the fine wordplay of *They Call Me Trinity* - the accent here is on the physical, with much lampooning of Westerns and religion. A poker game features a display of Trinity's nifty card shuffling (again speeded up and in some cases played backwards) and the local peones have black eyes because the drunken phoney monks beat them up after confession, giving them a shiner for absolution. Bambino visits the mission to test the theory and predictably ends up destroying the confessional booth. The finale of *Trinity Is Still My Name*, like its predecessor, is an extended punch-up, this time set in the mission, where Trinity and Bambino (dressed as monks) take on Parker's unarmed gang in a mass brawl. They are fighting over a money bag (referred to throughout by the monks as 'the root of all evil') and the whole sequence (an extended chase and fist fight) becomes an irreverent game of American Football, complete with monastic chanting on the soundtrack. For much of the film, Hill and Spencer are dressed in dapper suits and bowler-hats, further reinforcing their resemblance to Laurel and Hardy, and Hill's love interest is better integrated into the story. Here he falls for a pioneer girl called Wendy, played by the gorgeous Yanti Somer - his female equivalent, with blonde hair and vivid blue eyes. But unlike *They Call Me Trinity* absolutely no one gets killed here. This was obviously a conscious effort by Barboni to appeal to a younger fan base as well as to disenchanted Western fans, tired of bloodletting. It also explains why the movie quickly overtook Leone's movies as the most financially successful Spaghetti Western of all time. The appeal of the Trinity films transcends all ages, the silly humour can be appreciated by kids, the Western send-ups by their parents. Following the astronomical success of the Trinity movies, Hill and Spencer became the most bankable comedians in Europe, starring in knockabout comedies with exclamatory titles like *All The Way Boys!* (1972), *Watch Out, We're Mad!* (1973) and *Go For It!* (1983).

The Verdict: Many ersatz Trinity films followed, including the appalling *Jesse And Lester: Two Brothers In A Place Called Trinity* (1972) and Barboni resurrected the formula for the 1995 TV movie, *Trinity And Bambino: The Legend Lives On*, but none equalled the appeal of the first two movies. Their anarchic and childlike spirit is illustrated beautifully by Trinity's reasoning when he suspects foul play in Tescosa - "Parker gives us 4000 to close an eye and the Sheriff tells us to steer clear of a bunch of drunken monks. Something stinks here." 3/5

My Name Is Nobody (1973)

Director Tonino Valerii

Cast: Henry Fonda (Beauregard), Terence Hill (Nobody), Jean Martin (Sullivan)
115 minutes

Story: In 1899, notorious gunfighter Jack Beauregard decides it's time he retired. Age is catching up with him and he plans to travel to Europe, but he finds out that his brother has been killed by a corrupt businessman, Sullivan. So before he leaves the West, Beauregard sets out to claim his brother's share of a bogus gold mine that Sullivan has been running. Along the way Beauregard meets Nobody, a cocky young gunman, who hero-worships Beauregard and wants his idol to go down in history with a bang rather than retire quietly to Europe. He forces a confrontation between Beauregard and Sullivan's employees, the Wild Bunch - '150 pure-bred sons of bitches on horseback' - in the desert. Beauregard survives and in the finale Nobody kills him in a duel in the main street of New Orleans, before a huge crowd. But it transpires that the duel was a ruse to allow Beauregard to sail away in peace, having secured his place in history, and for Nobody to become famous. Now Nobody is a Somebody too.

Background: This film is often mistaken as a Sergio Leone film, but it was actually directed by Valerii, Leone's assistant from the Dollars movies and an excellent director in his own right (*Day Of Anger* and *The Price Of Power*). *My Name Is Nobody* is based on an idea by Leone and he produced it, though rumours that he directed much of the action seem to be largely unfounded. Like *Once Upon A Time In The West*, the film starred Fonda, but instead of a villainous role he is cast as the hero, an ageing gunslinger bound for Europe. Not only does Beauregard represent the end of the West - as the men who tamed the Wild West reached their twilight years - but also the end of the Classic Hollywood Western. Here he finds himself facing Nobody (though Trinity would have been a more accurate moniker) played by Hill, an impudent young gunman, full of verve and adventure, for whom Beauregard is a hero of gigantic proportions. Nobody represents the Spaghetti Western, the hip update of the old fables, which ironically was also on the way out by 1973, being ousted from the box office by Kung-Fu movies and Thrillers. Nobody wants Beauregard/ the Western to go down fighting, to leave a final testament that is a worthy legacy. Nobody tells Beauregard at one point, "A man who's a man needs something to believe in", and it was as though Leone and Valerii were saying that there was nothing to believe in any more. Stars like Eastwood and Van Cleef (men who owed their careers to Leone) had gone off and done their own thing and Trinity had come along and shot the great Leone myth full of holes, making a mockery of his once-cherished genre. Now Nobody was going to finish off the American Western, inasmuch as he was going to help it retire for good. Nobody finds himself at the end of the movie watching his back for the next generation of gunmen, eager to kill him off. Meanwhile at the box office, Bruce Lee and Darth Vader appeared and killed the Western off altogether.

My Name Is Nobody is a great Western, though it's not without its flaws. But let's not be too picky - to come up with anything original after the Trinity films had flogged the formula to death is commendable.

Valerii was accused of not being successful in linking the Italian and American styles together. But the point is that the two styles are so different that the pace of the film echoes their differing perspectives. The scenes with Fonda are more mannered, as befits an ageing 'National Monument' and have a twilight quality about them that anticipates the final attempt at resurrecting Spaghettis in the seventies with movies like *Keoma* - films full of regret and pathos. When Hill comes to the forefront, to perform his Trinity antics (slapping gunmen, drawing in double-quick time, eating beans) they juxtapose with Fonda's stately performance. But when the two are together, the power of their portrayals is extremely effective and the most touching depiction of the 'old man and boy' scenario from *For A Few Dollars More*. Nobody worships Beauregard and tells his hero, "When I was a boy I used to make believe I was Jack Beauregard", just as successive generations make believe they were Tom Mix, John Wayne, Alan Ladd and Clint Eastwood as they stared up at the cinema screen (and later TV). Ennio Morricone's score is similarly reverential, with nods to *A Fistful Of Dollars* and *Once Upon A Time In The West*, while the shoot-out between Beauregard and the Wild Bunch is scored with a pastiche of Wagner's 'Ride Of The Valkyries'. *My Name Is Nobody* was followed by an inferior sequel *A Genius* (1975) which was retitled *Nobody's The Greatest* and co-starred cult hero Patrick McGoohan (of sixties TV series *Danger Man* and *The Prisoner* fame).

The Verdict: After his shock casting as the villain in *Once Upon A Time In The West*, Fonda proved that he could play a bad guy, after years of heroic roles. Here Beauregard is a gentler, more optimistic version of John Wayne's J B Books in *The Shootist* (1976). *My Name Is Nobody* gave Fonda a role with grace and dignity that was also the perfect postscript to his Western career. Amazingly, it took the Italians to do it. 4/5

Keoma (1976)

Director Enzo G Castellari

Cast: Franco Nero (Keoma), Woody Strode (George), William Berger (Shannon), Donal O'Brien (Caldwell) 96 minutes

Story: After the Civil War half-breed Keoma returns to his home town to find it doubly cursed. The town is oppressed by a group of racist ex-Confederates led by Caldwell, while the population is riddled with the plague, which is rapidly decimating them. Keoma finds that his old mentor, George, is now the town drunk and his adopted father, Shannon, is powerless to stop Caldwell's tyranny, even though his three natural sons are members of Caldwell's outfit. Keoma saves a pregnant woman from the gang, but realises that he can't run away and must face his destiny. He convinces Shannon and George to help him and they face Caldwell's bunch, but George is killed, Caldwell murders Shannon and then takes Keoma prisoner. Meanwhile Keoma's three half-brothers see an opportunity to take over the town. They kill Caldwell and his men but Keoma escapes and kills them all in a showdown.

Background: Often praised as one of the greatest Spaghettis of all time, this isn't a patch on films from the heyday of the genre in 1965-67. That said, it is a very good Western, completely different in style to the classic Spaghettis and boasting a fine performance by Nero, in his best Western role outside his movies for Corbucci. The film belongs to the very last sub-genre to emerge from Italian Westerns - the so-called Twilight Westerns - before the genre finally capitulated shortly after *Keoma* was released. Its style was strange, mystical and Gothic, the story steeped in memory and narrated by mournful Leonard Coen-esque ballads on the soundtrack. But though it was very successful, *Keoma* failed to keep the genre afloat.

It is excellent in all departments, but one of the best aspects of the film is the trio of actors in the leads - Nero, Berger and Strode. Nero, looking nothing like his previous incarnations, gives one of his best performances as the half-breed Keoma. With a beard, long hair and a sawn-off shotgun, the film is an obvious attempt to shed his Django image once and for all, though it was marketed as a Django movie in some countries. Berger ages well, to play Keoma's stepfather, while Strode (who continued to make continental Westerns after his appearance in *Once Upon A Time In The West*) highlighted an anti-racist aspect to the action. The treatment of both the half-breed hero and his black mentor is simultaneously hard-hitting and topical and deals with themes already broached by Corbucci's *Navajo Joe*, amongst others. What makes the film even more unique is its startlingly innovative use of flashbacks. The usual style of the time was that the hero looked off into the distance, the screen dissolved and the reverie (usually sepia-tinted) would materialise from the blur. Though some of *Keoma*'s flashbacks are done that way, there are also moments where the memories seem part of the action so that when a character reminisces, the flashback takes place around him. Consequently, Keoma arrives back at his old home and in a surreal moment he watches himself as a child running past. Such instances add to the mystical and religious atmosphere, where the past and the present collide, in preparation for the future.

The film was also released as *The Violent Breed* and looking at the action sequences it's an apt title. Castellari (real name Enzo Girolami) emulated Peckinpah's approach to action scenes, with much slow-motion photography of bodies pirouetting as bullets slam into them, intercut with action shots at normal speed. This makes the set pieces memorable, especially when coupled with the very unusual setting and the extraordinary music. Other stylistic aspects involve some shamelessly contrived camerawork, including a scene where Nero and Berger are filmed through a series of bullet holes, as they shoot at a target - a simple enough masking effect that is enormously effective. The plague-infested town owes much to *Django*, and some of the action occurs at night, with the street atmospherically lit with torches. This bizarre imagery is made even weirder by the score by G & M De Angelis. Throughout the film a series of ballads comments on the action, but after a while their unrelentingly doom-laden tone begins to wear on the nerves. The male balladeer sounds like an even more gravelly-voiced version of Leonard Coen (whose laments had been used to similar effect in Robert Altman's *McCabe And Mrs Miller*), but his shrill female counterpart gets extremely irritating, though the fusion of music and image often produces undeniably powerful moments. *Keoma* is easily Castellari's best movie. In the sixties he made a career out of parodying Leone and pioneered the fusion of Spaghetti Western and comedy, but really came into his own with this mystical style. His scenario here is obviously heavily influenced by Bergman's *The Seventh Seal* (1957) - a soldier returning after his 'crusade' through a plague-wracked landscape. Throughout the film, Keoma repeatedly encounters two characters - an old woman and a young pregnant girl. The old woman appears at crucial moments in the film and signifies death, while the girl (symbolising life) gives birth during the final gunfight. As Keoma kills the town's oppressors (who have been stopping much needed medicine from reaching the infirm), her child is extremely fortunate to be the first born into a 'free world', while she perishes giving birth to him. As if to reinforce the religious element to the story, Keoma is symbolically crucified on a wagon wheel and Castellari is to be commended that he doesn't allow a totally upbeat ending.

The Verdict: A dark morality tale that manages to say something new at a time when it seemed that everything had been said. It also influenced Clint Eastwood's *Unforgiven* (1992), particularly the character of Ned Logan (played by Morgan Freeman) which is very similar to Strode's portrayal here. Nero is exceptionally proud of this film and rightly so. 4/5

If you haven't found your favourite Spaghetti then I'm sorry. Space dictated that it was impossible to cover more than 31 films and some inevitably fell by the wayside (goodbye *Today It's Me...Tomorrow You*, *Run Man Run*, *Sartana*, *Five Man Army* and *Django The Bastard*). The selected films are arranged roughly in chronological order for their original release in Italy. Running times relate to the most complete versions exhibited. The reason most inclusions score so highly in the ratings is that they are only the tip of the iceberg and (in my opinion) a fair representation of the genre's finest. I personally think that *The Good, The Bad And The Ugly* is the best Italian Western of all time, as well as one of the greatest Westerns. But ten more Spaghettis in a dead heat for second place are *The Return Of Ringo* (1965), *For A Few Dollars More* (1965), *The Big Gundown* (1966), *Django* (1966), *The Hills Run Red* (1966), *Navajo Joe* (1966), *The Big Silence* (1967), *A Professional Gun* (1968), *Sabata* (1969) and *They Call Me Trinity* (1970). It seems 1966 was a vintage year.

Reference Materials

Spaghetti Books

Sergio Leone - Something To Do With Death by Christopher Frayling (Faber and Faber 2000) The finest book on Leone's life and Westerns. Hugely informative, tirelessly researched. Definitive in every department. Buy it.

Italian Westerns - The Opera Of Violence by Laurence Staig and Tony Williams (Lorrimer 1975) Hard to find but worthy look at entire Spaghetti genre. Lots of stills, plus useful notes on composers.

Spaghetti Westerns by Christopher Frayling (Routledge and Kegan Paul 1981, reprinted 1998) The bible of Spaghetti Westerns. Mostly devoted to Leone's movies, but brings in Corbucci, Tessari and Sollima. Good filmography. Essential.

Sergio Leone by Oreste De Fornari (Gremese 1997) Good on-set stills and interesting interviews with Leone's associates including Morricone, Donati, Valerii.

Spaghetti Westerns - The Good, The Bad And The Violent. 558 Eurowesterns And Their Personnel, 1961-1977 by Thomas Weisser (McFarland 1992) Breathtaking in its scope. Massive and invaluable, but not infallible.

Western All'Italiana - The Specialists by Antonio Bruschini and Antonio Tentori (Glittering Images 1998) By far the most lavishly illustrated book on the subject (in colour!), but text let down by poor English translation. Good filmographies. Buy it for the pictures.

Once Upon A Time: The Films Of Sergio Leone by Robert C Cumbow (Scarecrow Press 1987) Leone-only analysis, but still very interesting.

Plus the excellent American fanzine **Westerns All'Italiana (editor Tom Betts)** and TV documentaries including *Viva Leone*, *Ennio Morricone* and *Once Upon A Time*.

Also fanzines on foreign cinema, LP booklets and the numerous biographies of **Clint Eastwood** (especially Patrick McGilligan, Iain Johnston, Francois Guerif and Daniel O'Brien) and **The Aurum Film Encyclopaedia - The Western by Phil Hardy** (which briefly covers all the main Spaghettis), **A Pictorial History Of Westerns by Michael Parkinson and Clyde Jeavons** (whole chapter, good stills) and **Wild West Movies by Kim Newman** (accessible, excellently researched).

Spaghetti Videos

Most of the films included here have been released on video in the UK in the past, but a pitifully small number of them are currently available. The good news is several video companies deal extensively in Italian Westerns. For example, you can drop Spaghetti specialist René Hogguer a line at Cinecity, PO Box 1710, 1200 BS Hilversum, The Netherlands or email Cinecity.Hogguer@WXS.NL for a catalogue.

A Fistful Of Dollars (1964), SO51796 (includes original trailer)
One Silver Dollar (1964), deleted
The Return Of Ringo (1965), GVO24 (as *The Angry Gun* - cut)
For A Few Dollars More (1965), SO56747 (includes original trailer)
A Bullet For The General (1966), deleted
The Good, The Bad And The Ugly (1966), SO54858 (cut, includes original trailer)
Django (1966), 6357863
The Hellbenders (1966), deleted
Death Rides A Horse (1967), SO54046
Face To Face (1967), deleted (some prints cut, also released as *High Plains Killer*)
Django Kill (1967), deleted (very cut)
Day Of Anger (1967), MMS1090 (as *Gunlaw* - very cut)
Once Upon A Time In The West (1968), VHR4197 (includes original trailer)
A Professional Gun (1968), deleted
The Price Of Power (1969), deleted
Sabata (1969), SO50614
Compañeros (1970), AKT4001 (cut)
A Man Called Sledge (1970), deleted
They Call Me Trinity (1970), deleted
Duck You Sucker (1971), deleted (released as *Fistful Of Dynamite* - cut)
Trinity Is Still My Name (1971), deleted
My Name Is Nobody (1973), deleted
Keoma (1976), deleted

The only way to see the most complete version of *The Good, The Bad And The Ugly* is to locate the Italian videotape or the UK/US DVD. *Seven Guns For The MacGregors*, *A Pistol For Ringo*, *Navajo Joe*, *A Stranger In Town*, *The Big Silence* and *Blindman* have been released on the continent on video. *Pistol*, *Navajo*, *Silence* and *Blindman* have been released in the US. But *The Big Gundown* and *The Hills Run Red* have only ever been shown on TV (*Hills* and *Gundown* have been shown on US Cable, while the short version of *Gundown* has been screened by FilmFour in the UK). For US format releases on video, check the Trash Palace at http://www.trashpalace.com/html/spaghetti_westerns.htm.

In addition to the above Spaghettis, the following key films referenced in this Pocket Essential have been available on video in the UK or Europe (on VHS), the US (on NTSC) or Japan (VHS and laserdisc). They are listed chronologically by their best-known title. Original release year, director and star in parenthesis.

The Treasure Of Silver Lake (1962, Harald Reinl/ Lex Barker)

Gunfight In The Red Sands/ Gringo (1963, Riccardo Blasco/ Richard Harrison)

Winnetou The Warrior/ Apache Gold/ Winnetou I (1963, Harald Reinl/ Lex Barker)

Bullets Don't Argue/ Pistols Don't Argue (1964, Mario Caiano/ Rod Cameron)

Last Of The Renegades/ Winnetou II (1964, Harald Reinl/ Lex Barker)

Among Vultures/ Frontier Hellcat (1964, Alfred Vohrer/ Stewart Granger)

Buffalo Bill - Hero Of The Far West (1964, Mario Caiano/ Gordon Scott)

Massacre At Canyon Grande/ Red Pastures (1964, Sergio Corbucci/ James Mitchum)

Minnesota Clay (1965, Sergio Corbucci/ Cameron Mitchell)

Viva Maria (1965, Louis Malle/ Brigitte Bardot)

For The Taste Of Killing/ Lanky Fellow (1966, Tonino Valerii/ Craig Hill)

Fort Yuma Gold/ The Rebel Lieutenant (1966, Giorgio Ferroni/ Giuliano Gemma)

The Handsome The Ugly The Cretinous (1966, Giovanni Grimaldi/ Franchi & Ingrassia)[never released in English language version]

Massacre Time/ Django The Runner/ The Brute And The Beast (1966, Lucio Fulci/ Franco Nero)

Ringo And His Golden Pistol/ Johnny Oro (1966, Sergio Corbucci/ Mark Damon)

Seven Women For The MacGregors/ Up The MacGregors (1966, Franco Giraldi/ David Bailey)

The Stranger Returns/ Shoot First Laugh Last/ A Man A Horse A Gun (1966, Luigi Vanzi/ Tony Anthony)

$10.000 Blood Money (1966, Romolo Guerrieri/ Gianni Garko)

Texas Adios/ The Avenger (1966, Ferdinando Baldi/ Franco Nero)

Three Golden Boys/ Death Walks In Laredo (1966, Enzo Peri/ Thomas Hunter)

The Tramplers (1966, Alfredo Antonini/ Joseph Cotton)

Bandidos (1967, Massimo Dallamano/ Enrico Maria Salerno)

Dead Or Alive/ A Minute To Pray A Second To Die (1967, Franco Giraldi/ Alex Cord)

God Forgives - I Don't/ Blood River (1967, Giuseppe Colizzi/ Hill & Spencer)

Little Rita Of The West/ Rita Kid (1967, Ferdinando Baldi/ Rita Pavone)

Man Pride Vengeance (1967, Luigi Bazzoni/ Franco Nero)

Requiescant/ Let Them Rest/ Kill And Pray (1967, Carlo Lizzani/ Lou Castel)

Seven Winchesters For A Massacre/ The Final Defeat/ Payment In Blood/ Blake's Marauders (1967, Enzo Girolami/ Edd Byrnes)

Wanted (1967, Giorgio Ferroni/ Giuliano Gemma)

Ace High/ Revenge At El Paso (1968, Giuseppe Colizzi/ Hill & Spencer)

Django Get A Coffin Ready/ Viva Django (1968, Ferdinando Baldi/ Terence Hill)

Kill Them All And Come Back Alone (1968, Enzo Girolami/ Chuck Connors)

Run Man Run (1968, Sergio Sollima/ Tomas Milian)

Today It's Me...Tomorrow You (1968, Tonino Cervi/ Brett Halsey)

White Comanche (1968, Jose Briz/ Joseph Cotton)

Boot Hill (1969, Giuseppe Colizzi/ Hill & Spencer)

Chuck Mool/ The Unholy Four (1969, Enzo Barboni/ Leonard Mann)

Django The Bastard/ Django The Avenger/ The Stranger's Gundown (1969, Sergio Garrone/ Anthony Steffen)

The Five Man Army (1969, Don Taylor/ Peter Graves)

Sartana/ If You Meet Sartana Pray For Your Death (1969, Gianfranco Parolini/ Gianni Garko)

The Silent Stranger/ Stranger In Japan (1969, Luigi Vanzi/ Tony Anthony)

Tepepa/ Blood And Guns (1969, Guilio Petroni/ Tomas Milian)

Adios Sabata/ The Bounty Hunters (1970, Gianfranco Parolini/ Yul Brynner)

The Forgotten Pistolero/ Gunmen Of Ave Maria (1970, Ferdinando Baldi/ Leonard Mann)

Heads I Kill You Tails You Die/ They Call Me Hallelujah (1971, Giuliano Carmineo/ George Hilton)

Long Live Your Death/ Don't Turn The Other Cheek/ Long Live Death...Preferably Yours (1971, Duccio Tessari/ Franco Nero)

The Return Of Sabata (1971, Gianfranco Parolini/ Lee Van Cleef)

Deaf Smith And Johnny Ears/ Los Amigos (1972, Paolo Cavara/ Franco Nero)

Jesse And Lester: Two Brothers In A Place Called Trinity (1972, Richard
   Harrison/ Richard Harrison)
What Am I Doing In The Middle Of A Revolution? (1972, Sergio Corbucci/
   Vittorio Gassman)
Blood Money/ Stranger And The Gunfighter (1973, Antonio Margheriti/ Lee
   Van Cleef)
A Genius/ Nobody's The Greatest (1975, Damiano Damiani, Terence Hill)

DVDs

Predictably, only the Dollars films are available on DVD at the
moment, though *Django* (with Franco Nero interview & trailer), *Day Of
Anger*, the 'Trinity' films, *My Name Is Nobody* and a Spaghetti Western
trailer disc have been released elsewhere.

Spaghetti Soundtracks

The soundtracks to almost all the main films included in this volume
have been released in full on vinyl LP. The ones that haven't are: *Seven
Guns For The MacGregors*, *A Stranger In Town*, *Death Rides A Horse*,
Django Kill, *Compañeros*, *A Man Called Sledge*, *Blindman*, *Trinity Is Still
My Name* and *Keoma*. The majority of vinyl has been deleted, but keep
your eyes peeled at film fairs and you never know what you may find.

Most of the films analysed in this book have also been released on CD,
but again there are exceptions. *Seven Guns For The MacGregors*, *The
Hills Run Red*, *Django Kill*, *Sabata*, *A Man Called Sledge*, *Blindman* and
Trinity Is Still My Name have never been out on CD. The CD versions of
Navajo Joe and *A Professional Gun* have very poor sound quality, so
beware.

The best Spaghetti compilation album is Ennio Morricone's *I Western*,
a triple LP boxed set which contains the title tracks to all Morricone's best
Westerns. Again deleted, even on CD. It's worth seeing some of Morricone's live concert videos, including *Live In Rotterdam*, *Cantata Per
L'Europe* and *Ennio Morricone At Santa Cecilia* (also available on CD).
And also look out for *Musica Sul Velluto*, a magazine on Morricone's
career, and *Il Giaguaro*, an Italian-language magazine devoted to the sixties and seventies music of Morricone and others. For expert soundtrack
information contact: lionel.woodman@talk21.com or Hillside CD Productions, Hillside House, 1 Woodstock Road, Strood, Rochester, Kent ME2
2DL.

Spaghetti Websites

There's a lot of stuff on the Net, with little of the depth of some of the books mentioned above. As you probably already know, the Internet Movie Database (**http://us.imdb.com**) is fantastic for filmographies and cast lists - for even the most obscure actor and film. See also:

http://www.film.tierranet.com/directors/s.leone/ - Leone's de facto homepage. A must-see site for fans, with excellent and well-attended message board, plus links, history, interviews and some images.

http://www.man-with-no-name.com/ - Clint's web page.

http://www.pscweb.com/macaroni/ - Spaghettis are called Macaroni Westerns in Japan. Good site, English language.

http://members.aol.com/ilcattivo2/ - Site devoted to Mr Ugly himself, Lee Van Cleef.

http://www.cinedelic.com/budterence/english/bud_terence.htm - Terence Hill and Bud Spencer proving their continued Euro popularity.

Plus a variety of sites on the genre, as both Spaghetti Westerns and Euro-Westerns (though beware that Eurowestern is also a political phrase which can cause confusion). Also fan pages on Giuliano Gemma, Tomas Milian and Franco Nero (with filmographies and pictures), poster galleries and fans reviews, availability of movies, soundtracks, favourites and opinions. The net's a good starting point, but there's no substitute for getting hold of some videos or soundtracks, tequila and a good cigar and sampling the Spaghetti Western atmosphere first-hand.